BISHOP OF THE RESISTANCE

Bishop of the Resistance

The Life of Eivind Berggrav, Bishop of Oslo, Norway

EDWIN ROBERTSON

CPH.
SAINT LOUIS

To Gunnar Heiene
Whose careful research brought Berggrav's story to life
first for Norwegians and now for the world.

All Scripture quotations, unless otherwise indicated, are taken from the King James Version of the Holy Bible.

Copyright © 2000 Edwin Robertson
Concordia Publishing House
3558 S. Jefferson Avenue, St. Louis, MO 63118-3968
Manufactured in the United States of America

Library of Congress Cataloging-in-Publication Data

Robertson, Edwin Hanton.
    Bishop of the resistance : a life of Eivind Berggrav, Bishop of Oslo, Norway / Edwin Robertson.
        p. cm.
    ISBN 0-570-05263-7
    1. Berggrav, Eivind, 1884-1959. 2. Lutheran Chruch—Norway—Bishops—Biography. 3. Church and state—Norway—History—20th century. 4. Norway—Church history—20th century. I. Title.
    BX8080.B43 R63 2001
    284.1′092—21   00-010384

1 2 3 4 5 6 7 8 9 10   09 08 07 06 05 04 03 02 01 00

Contents

Preface

In early May 1946, just one year after the end of the war in Europe, an international conference was held in England at a church house of the Chichester diocese. There plans for the United Bible Societies were laid: the national Bible Societies of the world would one day join together to pool their resources and work as one world body. Three men at that conference had worked closely together for years before the war, but this was their first meeting after a war that had torn their three countries apart—Britain, Germany, and Norway. From Britain, the Bishop of Chichester, the host George Bell; from Germany, Hanns Lilje, later to become Bishop of Hanover; and Bishop Eivind Berggrav of Oslo, Primate of Norway.

The harsh memories of the war that had separated them vanished quickly, as friendship and respect were immediately restored. Berggrav, who was to become the first President of the United Bible Societies, said of Bell: "Your name was a Christian symbol to us and how great was our gratitude towards you." During the five years of occupation by the German forces, Norway had seen Bell as, in Berggrav's words, "the bearer of something immensely valuable to us." "We have thanked God for you," he said, "and I think we should be allowed to thank you too."

Berggrav had called Bell a symbol, but Berggrav was also a symbol to many in Britain as he resisted the Nazi occupation with spiritual weapons. The third figure, Hanns Lilje of Germany, arrived late. Berggrav was seated in the chair, but as soon as he saw Lilje enter the room, he stood and walked the length of the room to embrace him.

These three champions of the fight against Fascism in all its forms held the attention of the conference. They represented the honorable struggle of the churches for justice, human rights, and the freedom of the church of Jesus Christ.

Throughout those long hard years in Britain, Bell had spoken out against National Socialism in Germany and spoken out for the care of refugees from Germany, for the internees during the war, for peace and, at the end of the war, a just and honorable settlement with Germany. For this he suffered abuse and humiliation at the hands of his countrymen and others, and the door to higher office in the Church of England was shut. But in occupied Europe and among the resisters in Germany itself, he was a symbol of hope.

Hanns Lilje was a part of the German resistance and had been released only a year before from a Nazi prison by the American forces.

Yet the man whose story is the theme of this book, Eivind Berggrav, was for three years (1942–1945) under house arrest in his own cabin in Asker, some miles away from Oslo. Despite his arrest and confinement, he led the church in its resistance to domination by the Quisling State. In various disguises—policeman, businessman, at times even sporting a false moustache—and often with the connivance of his guards, he made many journeys to meet other church leaders and plan the strategy of resistance. He was not executed largely because of the representation made by Helmuth Von Moltke and Dietrich Bonhoeffer on their visit to Norway during the German occupation.

After Berggrav's death in 1959, Hanns Lilje remarked of his friend, "Eivind Berggrav was one of the few truly great figures of recent church history. He was very prudent and very courageous, a Christian with a deep and simple faith, and at the same time a man of great immediacy who could effortlessly come close to people."

A short time before Berggrav died, Sverre Smaadahl of the Norwegian Bible Society took me to spend a few hours with him in the same cabin where he had been under house arrest. I had known Berggrav for some years and worked with him in the United Bible Societies, of which at the time I was Study Secretary. We did not talk about the Bible Societies, but he reminisced during our visit.

He recalled from the war the young German guards who often stood outside in the cold. He invited them in, and soon they were showing him photographs of their children and telling him of their homesickness. In his younger days he had been a prison chaplain. Now the prisoner was chaplain to his guards! Human relationships overtook the hatred of war.

When the puppet government under Quisling attempted to interfere with the proper role of the church and tried to mobilize the youth of the country into a Nazi youth movement, Berggrav called the church out on strike. First the bishops resigned their offices. Afterward almost the entire clergy of the country resigned on Easter Day 1942, giving up their salaries and leaving their official residences.

The church under Berggrav's leadership resisted without violence and the people followed the clergy. When a Nazi sympathizer was appointed to the historic Cathedral in Trondheim, the people stood outside in thousands while the new Dean entered a more or less empty cathedral. Outside, the German soldiers stood guard while the crowd sang Luther's hymn, "A Safe Stronghold Our God Is Still" ("A Mighty Fortress Is Our God") including the words:

> If they take our life
> Goods, honor, child and wife—
> Let everything go:
> They have no profit so;
> The kingdom ours remaineth.

> (*Luther's Works* 53:285)

Some said that there were tears in the eyes of the German soldiers, many of whom were Lutherans and loved that hymn.

Perhaps Berggrav embroidered the story as he told it to me that day; but that was the manner of his resistance: spiritual resistance with spiritual weapons.

Acknowledgements

In 1992, a definitive biography of Eivind Berggrav (Bishop of Oslo and Primate of Norway when Germany invaded his country) was published by the University Press of Oslo. The author, Gunnar Heiene, had thoroughly researched all the available manuscripts and consulted with relevant scholars and former acquaintances of the bishop. It was handsomely produced with illustrations. That book provides much of the material used in the present volume. Vandenhoeck and Ruprecht of Göttingen published a shortened and edited German edition in 1997. Bishop Berggrav's international contacts and the leading role he played in church relations, quite apart from the fascinating story of the way he led church and people in legitimate resistance to the occupying forces, required an English version.

It is reported that when the Norwegian and German editions were shown to a British publisher with the request that he publish an English translation, he took a volume down from his shelves and said: "Look! We cannot sell the biography of an English bishop. How can we expect to sell a foreign one?" The shock of that reply led us to think, not of a straight translation of the German or Norwegian work, but a total rewriting of the material for an English-speaking readership.

My task was, therefore, to read the two books, meet with Gunnar Heiene, as well as those in Norway who had assisted him, examine the archives of research material, and finally write a biography which would be more accessible to the English-speaking world.

I have tried to present this Norwegian bishop who was my friend and a close colleague in such a way that the reader would want to know him and would appreciate what he did, thought, and said as still relevant to the problems facing us today.

Two other books have been of particular value in recasting the material: Alex Johnson, who was a contemporary of Berggrav and a close friend and colleague, wrote a brief biography *Eivind Berggrav: Spenningens Mann (Man of Tensions)*, published by Land og Kirke, Oslo. Vandenhoeck and Ruprecht, Göttingen subsequently translated the book into German and published it in 1960.

The other book was written by Richard Petrow, *The Bitter Years* (London: Hodder & Stoughton, 1974). This latter was of particular value with its details of the military campaigns.

Shortly before this manuscript was finished a third book (an English translation of a Norwegian orginal) was published that caused me to add a substantial section on Quisling; see Hans Fredrik Dahl, *Quisling* (ET; Cambridge: Cambridge University Press, 1999).

It is from these volumes that quotations are taken.

I am grateful to Handsel Press (Edinburgh, Scotland) and Concordia Publishing House (St. Louis, Missouri, United States) for undertaking the publication of an English account of a courageous Norwegian.

Edwin Robertson

Prologue

In August 1958, a few months before his death, Bishop Eivind Berggrav invited me to his cabin in Asker, north of Oslo. A summer chalet that he had purchased for his family as a retreat from the pressures of a bishop's life, the cabin was also his home during his years of house arrest (1942–45). The Quisling government regarded the Bishop of Norway as the most dangerous man in the German-occupied nation.

Berggrav talked at length with his usual humor, though the signs of his illness were evident. He began with his standard joke as he held his long pipe: years before his father had warned him to stay away from tobacco, so Eivind bought the longest pipe he could find. But the Bishop quickly came to the point of our time together. He was interested in telling his story, the story of three years of solitary confinement. He was closely guarded and the guards were severely warned not to consort with him. But with his kindness and charm, Eivind Berggrav was soon able to win over the soldiers. He called them "the good guards," and he was most careful to note when they were on duty. With their help, he managed to visit some of his neighbors, even celebrating his birthday in a friend's house nearby.

Although these years were lonely and any breach of confinement was likely to be punished, Eivind found ways of getting out of his home without notice. The newly "appointed"

Minister President Quisling wanted to put Berggrav to death as a traitor, but powerful friends in Berlin prevented Quisling from acting. (In truth, Berlin "pulled the strings" of this puppet ruler.) But it was dangerous for any guard to help Berggrav and the Bishop himself took great risk when he went away from his prison. In fact, he made several trips to Oslo, meeting with fellow conspirators in a committee of resistance. These meetings enabled Berggrav to maintain a sense of control on the resistance. He held together men of all theological persuasions—from fundamentalists to liberals—in the common cause of preventing Nazi ideology from perverting the church. His resistance, always non-violent, was effective as bishops and clergy came together in those dark times.

Berggrav recounted meetings held in the cabin itself. An early achievement was to secure privacy. One night before retiring to bed, he took a huge log and flung it with all his might into the surrounding woods. The noise was obvious, deliberate. It attracted the attention of the guards and they thought their prisoner was escaping. They searched the woods but soon returned to the cabin, breaking down the door. As they entered the house, they found Berggrav at the top of the stairs, in his long night shirt, protesting: "It is not enough that you have a company of soldiers to keep an old man penned up in this cabin. Now you invade the privacy of his bedroom!"

The captain of the guards was crest-fallen; he apologized and promised that no guard would again enter the cabin. This, of course, is exactly what Berggrav wanted. Because of these new "arrangements," friends could be smuggled into the cabin and not be detected. Colleagues could bring news of the resistance and hear his advice on plans—the very things Quisling wanted to prevent! The Minister President knew Berggrav's reputation and influence, and bitterly resented his role in keeping the church opposed to the government. Quisling even tried to bribe Berggrav, offering freedom if the Bishop left the country. Berggrav may have been tempted to leave, but when he received word that the King wanted him to stay in Norway (because he could do more harm to the occupation in his cabin than he could in England with the government-in-exile), he refused all further offers of rescue or release.

As we talked together that day in 1958, we both sensed that our visit may well be our last. We had been close colleagues in the cause of Bible reading and distribution around the world and naturally we reminisced about our efforts together. Eivind Berggrav did much during his confinement as well as after the war to produce a quality translation of the Holy Scriptures in Norwegian.

Like his experience during the occupation, Berggrav's life was, at times, difficult and filled with change. He acquired his character and commitment to his faith through many obstacles. He made mistakes, to be sure, but he also knew how to admit his mistakes and to take corrective action. Yet two truths provided him with a solid rock for his life's work: 1) his belief in the Bible as the Word of God, and 2) his conviction that Luther's insights into Christ and the Gospel were fundamental for the church. He often remarked, "In times of war and occupation, the Bible is a clear light to what should be done; but in times of prosperity it becomes a very difficult book." Under house arrest he offered a powerful defense of Luther against those who were using the Reformer to support anti-Semitism. These two themes, Scripture and God's grace in Christ, interwined to focus his life and ministry. They remained his hope and comfort in the hour of his death.

1

A Faith Forged in Doubt

The future Bishop of Oslo was born on October 25, 1884, the son of Otto Jensen, a schoolmaster at the time, who had come to Stavanger in 1883. Eivind's father was the major influence in his life. His mother, Marena, had married a sea captain when she was quite young. Her first husband died after 18 years of marriage; they had no children. When Otto Jensen arrived in Stavanger, he took Marena, ten years older than him, into his home as housekeeper. Soon the relationship deepened and they were married. As influential as Marena was in the home, Otto was the dominant personality in the lives of their three children: Eivind, the oldest, a sister, Ellen Margarethe, and a younger brother, Birger Alexander. The younger brother was sickly and could not join in the boisterous childhood games. As a result, Eivind developed a very close relationship to his sister. His most important, however, and in many respects enigmatic, relationship was with Otto Jensen. Oscar Pfister, an intimate of Sigmund Freud, a Protestant pastor in Switzerland and a psychoanalyst, once said to Berggrav in 1933, "Your father is the figure of destiny in your life." And so it proved. The younger Eivind struggled long to separate himself from his father, but never quite succeeded. In death, the father was even more powerful. To understand Eivind Berggrav is to begin with his father Otto Jensen.

OTTO JENSEN

Otto Jensen was born September 11, 1856, in Konigsberg, the youngest son of Even Jensen. His father was prominent in the church as a layman, often called "The Verger." His wife, Inger Margrethe Berggrav, whose family had come from Saxony in the 18th century, brought the German name of Berggrav into the family. These grandparents meant a great deal to the young Eivind and in later years he took the name of Berggrav. At first he joined it to Jensen, but a Norwegian law required him to choose one or the other. He chose Berggrav and that is how the world now knows him.

Otto Jensen, like his son, inherited an admiration for Germany. It was there that he developed his theology. His student days fell within the period in which Norway "broke through" into modern times. The impulse of modern science and radical biblical criticism surged through the nation and its universities. The strife between strict orthodox theology and a new practical theology greatly influenced the theological students even in Christiania (now Oslo) where Otto Jensen studied. In 1880, this freshly minted and polyglot student of theology, together with a student friend, toured the famous universities of Germany and absorbed much. But still Jensen felt at home in the more orthodox schools. It was suggested that he study Philosophy of Religion and qualify as an academic. Nothing came of this, though, and like many theological students, he chose teaching as a career. He was, however, a qualified theologian, and as late as 1898 had his dissertation on "Sin and Forgiveness" accepted by the faculty at Christiania.

Otto Jensen remained a teacher in Stavanger for six years, while the young Eivind grew. Then an abrupt change occurred. In 1889, Otto Jensen was called to a charge in Berg and became chaplain of the daughter-church in Asak. The family remained there for ten years. It was totally different from Stavanger and the children were delighted by it. In his "Memories of Childhood," Berggrav wrote, "Asak became my home and I loved it."

LIFE IN ASAK

In Asak Eivind felt free, no longer confined by his family. He spent much time in the open air, away from town and in the country. The young boy now enjoyed many more opportunities for outdoor activities and play with his sister and the children of the villages. In his free time, Eivind enjoyed exploring everything—the parsonage, the neighboring homes, the woods and meadows. But a three-meter high waterfall made the greatest impression. With this waterfall, the ten-year-old Eivind had an experience that influenced his whole attitude to life. He described this event years later.

> It was quite simple: suddenly, after I had been there many times, watching the water cascading over the little hill, I began to search over the top of the waterfall and beyond. Then I made up my mind to explore what lay beyond the waterfall. There was an area of woodland, so that at first I could not trace the river, which fed the waterfall, because it disappeared, round a bend into the forest. Without thinking, I explored further, asking myself what lies behind that bend in the river? I went on, crossing a field and searching until I came to a hill in the midst of the wood, which until then I had not been able to see, I had discovered where the river came from.

The ten-year-old was left wondering and excited that he had discovered the source of the waterfall. Thirty years later, he used this experience in his dissertation. It was not just an illustration, but a detailed personal experience to establish his thesis that the human spirit has a longing to reach out beyond its limitations.

The young Eivind Jensen showed a talent for organization and leadership qualities. He was always active. His father was not given to praise (a trait he inherited from his own father), so Eivind took great encouragement from a conversation he overheard between his father and the family doctor: "The youngster is always busy with something, and much of it works out. Certainly he will one day make something of himself." Later, Eivind commented in his memoirs, "Nothing in my whole life has meant more to me than these words of my father to the family doctor."

Asak, in the Østfold, near to the Swedish border, was an idyll that could not last. Its impressions remained with Eivind: the influence of the Haugian evangelical movement and the new revival movement from western Sweden. But the family had financial problems in Berg. The post of chaplain at Asak was not lucrative and Otto Jensen accepted an invitation to the branch church of St. Peter's in Stavanger. So they returned and Eivind's childhood came to an end when they left Østfold. The children were not pleased about the change. In his memoirs Berggrav is quite descriptive: "I longed to return, from that moment I hated Stavanger." After ten years in the east of Norway, in a rural community, he found the town life of Stavanger on the west coast totally different. As the years passed he became even more aware of the religious differences between the east and the west of his country.

YOUTH IN THE STAVANGER YEARS

In 1900, Eivind Jensen was enrolled in the Gymnasium and began serious study. In the same year he was confirmed by his father. These two events brought a theological tension. That autumn Eivind changed. Instead of accepting passively what he was told, he questioned everything, reflecting upon the beliefs and practices he observed around him. Natural science caught his attention; the logic of the scientific captivated and never left him. To any young student in 1900, the achievements of science were bound to be attractive. However, the religious controversies of the day, which at that time were tear-ing the church apart, also absorbed his attention. Religion and science came together under the influence of Thorvald Klaveness, a lively pastor who coined the slogan, "Free Science on a Christian Basis." Here was an opportunity to combine a living Christian faith with acceptance of the achievements of science. Subsequently, Eivind's first dissertation for the Gymnasium was "The Christian Religion and its Relation to the Thinking of the Educated Young." While trying to come to terms with the pietistic teaching he had met in Stavanger, he described two recognized psychological types: the emotional and the realistic. He placed himself solidly among the latter. But the realist in him did not prevent Eivind from building on a religious foundation. In this dissertation he wrote:

> We must believe that something exists over all the secrets of nature, that there is a higher power, which rules over the powers of nature and can place all the powers of nature in its service.

His theology was the fruit of struggle and resolution. Even when he was questioning most earnestly, he was active in the Christian Union of students and leading Bible study groups. He was a believing and growing Christian, who learned more than he admitted from the pietism of Stavanger with its strong missionary emphasis. From missionary talks he learned that there was a place in Christian discipleship for moral responsibility and cultural tasks, as well as the acceptance of Christ as Victor in the struggle against evil.

At the Gymnasium at Stavanger, he saw his vocation clearly. He would follow in the steps of his father, study theology and become a pastor.

THE STUDENT YEARS

Shortly before his 19th birthday, Eivind Jensen began his theological studies in the University of Christiania (Oslo). For the first time he lived away from home in a student hostel. At this time the church itself was in turmoil. Liberals and conservatives contended for the places of leadership in the church and for the significant theological chairs at the university. The years 1902–1905 would see a revolutionary change in the Church of Norway and the changes echoed in the mind of the young students. Most took sides in the controversies. There were stout defenders of the faith as delivered to their fathers and there were restless spirits determined to drag the church into the twentieth century. Eivind Jensen lived on both sides of the divide. Like his father, he held an orthodox view in theology, but tolerance in politics. As the strife in the church increased, Eivind found himself differing from his father. This may partially explain why he added Berggrav to his name in 1907. There were deep changes in his views as he combined vigorous evangelical activity among the students with constant questioning of his faith. He found expression for his questioning in journalism, a profession he admired all his life.

Already in his first year at university, Eivind established himself as a correspondent for the *Stavanger Aftenblad*. By the spring of 1904 he was able to keep his west-Norwegian readers up-to-date with the disputes among the professors in Christiania. His father was also involved in these controversies. Eivind wrote fluently, avoiding rigid categorization. He could always see and understand different points of view. The strife among his teachers made him wary of hard and fast theological lines. His experiences at this time explain why throughout his life Berggrav avoided categorical statements on theology and remained on good terms with people on different sides of any argument. This pattern was also true, for different reasons, of his period with the Bible Society, as well as in his leadership in the resistance to the German occupation.

ROBERT WILDER

Eivind Berggrav-Jensen was noticed as an enthusiastic worker in Christian student groups. He was soon involved in the World Student Christian Federation (WSCF), formed by

John R. Mott in 1895 at Vadstena, Sweden. The man who brought the WSCF to Norway, Robert Wilder, had a powerful influence on Berggrav. They met at a conference in Denmark and Eivind soon fell under the influence of this missionary preacher. In the autumn of 1903, the surge of interest among Scandinavian students in Bible and Prayer Groups was largely due to Wilder's influence. For Berggrav, these contacts had important consequences. For a time he was fascinated by the intensity and inner strength that Wilder displayed. In later years he described Wilder as a perceptive preacher who could read the hearts of people so that they became like wax in his hands. In Wilder, he encountered a form of personal Christianity, rooted in the revival movement of Moody and Sankey. In particular Eivind was attracted by Wilder's spiritual Bible studies, in which an allegorical method of interpretation was used, taking the message straight to the heart, rather than merely the mind. Using this American model, Berggrav prepared a prayer diary, accompanied by prayer themes for each morning and evening. He used it with the student group he was now leading. Eivind seemed confident and convinced, but behind the facade there were dangerous rifts in his faith.

The most evident rift was the contradiction between his Christian activity and his theological studies. Students brought up in evangelical homes will often find difficulties reconciling the two worlds. Some may lose their faith. At this time, Berggrav did not, but there was no doubt that his enthusiasm for the Bible (which Wilder had awakened) belonged to a totally different world from that of his biblical studies in the university. The tension between these two worlds threatened to tear him apart.

JOHN R. MOTT

The climax came in 1905 when Eivind was chosen to be a member of the Norwegian delegation to the World Congress of the World Student Christian Federation in Zeist. The Norwegian group traveled together and among the participants was Kathrine Seip. The students made a tour of their delegation, stopping at Dresden, Berlin, and taking part in a student mission in the University of Halle. In Zeist, they met one of the most outstanding Christian leaders of the day: John R. Mott. Wilder attended the Congress and greeted Eivind warmly, but it was John Mott who made the deeper impression. In particular, Berggrav was struck by Mott's emphasis on the importance of Bible study, prayer *and* social work. Only those who met the man could really appreciate the considerable impact of his powerful and energetic personality. He often spoke about the "four-square man" and looked the part. Massive in frame, Mott always appeared as one who knew where he was going. Stephen Neill writes of him "he seemed often to have the force of a battleship moving effortlessly through the water. Mott could never speak in any terms other than the superlative. For him every hour was the decisive hour." It was no surprise that students like Eivind, full of questions and doubts, found Mott stimulating and convincing.

During one of the sessions, John Mott asked the students to jot down on a piece of paper how much they could collect in their own country, with God's help, to support Christian action. Eivind was full of enthusiasm and wrote down 1000 kroner (approximately 400 U.S. dollars). Then he looked at one of the other students from Norway and saw that he had written only 15! In his memoirs Berggrav adds, "I had already curbed my enthusiasm down to 200, but he had only 15, so I contented myself with 50."

While most students at the Congress were talking about the separation of Norway from Sweden in nationalistic terms, Eivind, as nationalistic as his father, was more deeply concerned with a religious crisis that threatened to destroy his faith. At first, back in Christiania, it did not seem to matter much that the energetic Christian leader of the students, Eivind Jensen, had doubts about his beliefs. But beneath the multiple activities and involvements of his Christian social work, the old question that troubled his schooldays still lived on: "Had modern science not long since weakened the Christian dogmas?"

THE CRISIS AT HOME

In 1906, Eivind's relationship to his father altered radically. In the turmoil of strife within the church, Otto Jensen, now senior minister in the church at Skjeberg, was invited by the Prime Minister to accept the office of Minister of Religion and Education. This he did and the family moved to Christiania. Eivind now lived at home.

The presence of his parents in Christiania did nothing to alleviate his religious brooding. His father was too busy to help him and he knew that any discussion with his fellow students would bring only superficial answers to his problems. But what had been personal and private now inevitably became known to his family. His diary at that time traces his struggle. In these notes he busied himself with constant self-analysis, which had the effect of paralyzing his studies. To overcome this he separated his academic work from his personal beliefs and became a kind of "split-personality." He felt himself to be "poorer in spirit," seriously provoked by the radical stance of Søren Kierkegaard. He longed for a "confident feeling" in his personal and spiritual life, but it was contradicted by what he thought to be the reality of science. The diary entries tell of continuing doubts and by the end of April, 1906, these inner tensions affected even his style of writing. He wanted to retain the conservative theology which had thrown him into these doubts, but he could neither rest at peace with his old beliefs nor find any satisfaction in a radical theology. He was fully aware of the danger of his situation.

> I have become skeptic about everything. The split in my mind has grown so wide that I can wander from one part into the other when I want to.

This could not continue. One evening in June, his religious faith had reached its lowest point. After hours of discussion with a neighboring lawyer, Carl J. Hambro, who later became President of the Norwegian Parliament, Eivind walked home alone deeply troubled. He could not sleep and later recorded the thoughts that passed through his head at the time. He wrote, among other comments, that a voice spoke within him. "This is the hour of the death of your faith," it said. "From now on you are a free-thinker." Eivind the student was now a freethinker, but he had not abandoned his theological studies. It seemed more important now than ever that he should work more earnestly at theology because he had broken with faith. All barriers were down and there was no issue that could not be discussed and critically examined with an open mind.

Although Berggrav was now a freethinker, he was not convinced that "anything goes." Good and evil remained as realities. He had broken with the Christian faith, but not with Christian morality. He saw his problem as intellectual and he could not accept the solution of combining both the scientific explanation of the world and the religious explanation of behavior if it were based upon a "false" understanding of the world.

The problem, of course, was not entirely intellectual. It was also an emotional reaction to the kind of "enthusiastic religion" he had met in the Christian Union and an inner conflict with his father.

He did not at once break with the Christian Union of students, nor did he confess his loss of faith to his father. Outwardly, he went on as though nothing had changed. In July 1906, a month after that crucial night of "the death of his faith," he was actively engaged with the Nordic Christian Student Movement in Nyslott (Finland). He was a member of the committee preparing the conference and the obvious leader of the Norwegian group to go to Finland. Inwardly, Berggrav felt that he no longer "belonged," not socially but spiritually. His fellow students noticed nothing. They asked him to stand as a candidate for President of the Christian Union. He refused, but did not give his reasons. The inner break registered no outer change. He was still friendly and popular, but spiritually Eivind was alone.

EIVIND AND HIS FATHER

In August 1906, Eivind came face-to-face with his father in sacramental worship. Otto had been asked to preach at a student conference. Eivind went to the altar with his student friends and received the sacraments. It may have been an attempt to revive his faith, but that was not the effect. Returning to Christiania in the train he dug deep into his Bible, hoping to find a way out, but this hope came to nothing. Some years would pass before he went again to the altar to receive the sacraments. The crisis went deep and was very painful. The bitterness against Christian faith became a hatred of the Bible. He thought of burning the Confirmation Bible which his mother had given him. Symbolically, he tore out the page on which she had written and burnt it. Eivind Berggrav's faith was dead.

Back at the university, a small group of students who were less demonstrative than the others formed what they called "The Family." This group of eight young people sustained him and of it he wrote, "Here each could live as I lived. One was not observed by searching eyes and there were no snide remarks."

KATHRINE SEIP

Among these new friends, one soon held a special place. Born March 23, 1883, Kathrine Seip was a year and a half older than Eivind. He met her first on student work in 1904, some time before they developed a close and trusting relationship. Kathrine was the daughter of a pastor. After a year as governess in her uncle's household (1901), she had come to the capital city to study science and mathematics. Quite early Eivind saw her as clever and competent in all she did. With her he began to understand his objections to the form of Christianity which had become more and more strange and unacceptable to him, but he also began to see the possibility of rational and convincing alternatives.

For two years he saw his relationship with Kathrine grow and deepen in the group they called "The Family." When they were separated by Eivind's studies in Marburg (April to July 1907), they grew even closer by correspondence. Their letters were frequent and dealt with personal and profound questions about faith and lifestyle. Kathrine understood his difficulties with faith; she had herself gone through the same testing period. Some time later, she said to him that she had decided to go to China as a missionary. Suddenly, Eivind saw his world collapse. He blurted out, "I simply could not imagine life without you. If you decide to go to China, I will come with you."

They were soon engaged. Eivind's difficulties with faith and theology did not disappear, but now he could discuss them openly with one he loved and trusted. Later, he confessed that during this time he wrote to her, "like a small child, as to a mother, mature and understanding, seeking comfort."

How different his father's response was when at last Eivind plucked up the courage to write to him from Marburg to confess that he had lost his faith and could not be a pastor. His father was patient and practical. "Would it not be better," he said, "to give up theology and undertake a course in engineering." He suggested the Technical University in Berlin. Eivind did not take his advice.

ANALYSIS BY LETTER

During the two-year engagement period, Eivind and Kathrine were mostly separated. Eivind was in Marburg again for the spring and summer of 1908. After a brief meeting in the autumn, Kathrine was traveling, first in Cambridge and then back to Marburg. Their correspondence, which was considerable, provides the best account of his spiritual wrestling. His letters to Kathrine contrast sharply with the formal letters he wrote to his parents.

Kathrine was a good observer and sensitive to the nuances of Eivind's slightest reference. The expression of his feelings swung from happy optimism to the deepest doubts; Kathrine was able to follow him as much in the heights as in the depths. The idea that he had chosen a definite and singular vocation in one letter could change to despair and uncertainty in the next. She perceived that Eivind was often afraid of his own innermost thoughts and feelings.

In 1907 Eivind saw a performance of Goethe's "Faust" at a theatre in Berlin. He never forgot the impact of that great work and its echo in his own troubled soul. It was in that period, when his thoughts centered so intensely on his own development, that his life-long interest in psychology was awakened. He was introspective, studying the innermost corners of his soul. What emerged was evidence of his own motives and emotions. He explored with frightening confidence and began to think of himself as one who really knew, especially about his own inner motivation:

> I believe my psychological knowledge to be greater than that of the poet or the scholar. I seek out the inner hidden spaces of my soul, not methodically, not intuitively, but by sudden inspiration.

After that burst of confidence he gave up and, writing to Kathrine in Cambridge, said, "Can we not rather write of everyday things, just for ourselves and cease for a while discussion of the great problems of life?"

ON THE WAY BACK TO FAITH

Although Eivind did not take his father's advice and study engineering in Berlin, with his father's financial support he did seek help outside Norway. "In our country, theology is narrow and bitter," his father had said. "When you get out you will widen your horizon." Berggrav's time in Marburg, both the spring of 1907 and the autumn of 1908, was of great importance for the recovery of his faith. On the way to Marburg, he took courage in both hands and sought out Harald Høffding. They had a very open and personal conversation, after which Høffding said, in unforgettable words, "The religious question, my young friend, is never solved. But life would not be worth living if this question was not there."

At Marburg he spoke freely with this teachers, many of them the most renowned in Europe. In the autumn of 1908, he did not do too well in his examinations and the faint hope of an academic career became fainter.

But it was in Marburg that he began his journey back to faith. In one short paragraph, Alex Johnson describes this pilgrimage:

> During this time (in Marburg) the question of his faith weighed heavily upon him and led to a positive issue: why do I believe when I look at the world as a whole, and why have the materialists got it wrong? The answer he reached after much searching was that all human life without spirit is poor and of little worth, a failure if it consists only of human bodies and their laws. He concluded that spirit is an independent reality, which cannot be derived from natural laws. He had learnt that from Høffding. And while he assessed the characteristics of the world of the spirit, its own laws, its claims and ideals, "which in the important things of life are the same for everybody," he came to God.

In a letter to a friend, Eivind wrote, "Within the material world, I recognize the spirit as reality, and within the world of the spirit, on the other hand, the knowledge of sin is the great and sure reality." Alex Johnson comments, "On these two foundation stones [Berggrav] built his house." Although Eivind's stop in Copenhagen to visit Harald Høffding had a great influence upon him, his time in Marburg was decisive. There he learned much from the lectures of Wilhelm Herrmann, and even more from conversations with him as they took long walks. From one of these conversations came the advice: "Respond to your experiences and you will find your way." Herrmann was a liberal theologian, but what was central to his faith was an experience of Jesus Christ.

Another aspect of Herrmann's theology, which appealed to Berggrav, was the strong emphasis he put on ethical seriousness. In these lectures, Berggrav found the arguments for his resistance to the form of Christianity that he had known since his childhood. He commented that in this pietism the connection between religion and ethics had been in short supply! Berggrav had come a long way, but there was still a long way to go. He had to reconcile religion and life. He began the journey through his journalism.

Writer and Journalist

As a writer Eivind Berggrav began to explore the lives of great men, like Nansen and Amundsen, brave and leading personalities. This searching was expressed in a series of biographical articles. He also began to write literary reviews. At this time he was quite scornful of the "dirty business of politics," but was not without his own political views. His father was by now a politician (Minister of Religion and Education in the Government) and this did not improve Eivind's opinion of politicians.

One question more than others triggered his own political activity. It was the German involvement in South Jutland and North Schleswig. In Marburg, Berggrav met a Dane, Ott Ravn, who had been much concerned with the fight against German oppression of the Danish people in South Jutland. In order to see for himself, Berggrav went home from Marburg via the Danish and German border country. He made a study of the situation, but although he interviewed some Danes they would not let him quote them in the article for *Morgenblad* for fear of reprisals. At first, his standpoint had been conservative, but the behavior of the reactionary Prussians shocked him and turned his sympathy to the Liberals. Eivind was never, however, a thorough radical.

These student years shaped the rest of his life. He learned to pose radical questions, discovered sides of his own personality that were new to him, and made a journey back to a more secure foundation for life. These years also laid the foundation for his considerable work in journalism and as a writer. Few bishops have been able to edit, report, draft, or publish better than Berggrav.

2

A Question of Vocation

His student days over, Eivind Berggrav, like many other young men, decided upon his future career. October 25, 1908, was his twenty-fourth birthday. He had a bewildering number of interests, any of which could have led to a career. His father was not so foolish as one may think when he suggested that Eivind should study engineering in Berlin. From his childhood he had shown a scientific bent—inventing and experimenting, always with an insatiable curiosity. He was also an excellent speaker and enjoyed public presentations. His leadership qualities were becoming more and more evident. He had developed a strong interest in psychology and also in theories of teaching. Most obvious of all was his skill as a journalist. Yet over all these career options hung the shadow of his father and the ambivalent call to a pastorate.

THE TEACHER

In his thoughts about the future, Eivind had to consider Kathrine and how they would make a life together. Early in 1909, something happened that almost led to a decision. The newspaper, *Morgenblad*, sent him to Eidsvoll, some fifty miles north of Christiania, to cover the opening of a new Folk High

School. It was a wonderful and fateful assignment. Even the weather played its part—a sparkling winter day in the middle of January. There he heard Olaus Arvesen give the main address. Forty-four years before, Arvesen, together with Herman Anker, had formed the first Folk High School in Hamar, Norway. Apart from reviewing the development of the Folk High School movement in Norway, Arvesen spoke of the ideas of Grundtvig in Denmark upon which the movement was based. What attracted Berggrav most about this was the effect it had had upon the village communities in Denmark and the emphasis on teaching by the spoken word. He was fascinated by the whole movement and began to see his vocation as a teacher within it.

On the night train back to Christiania, he wrote a letter to Kathrine, who was far away in Marburg, telling her of his enthusiasm for the Folk High School and his conversation with Jon Sørensen. He added, almost parenthetically, "How would you like to manage a High School?"

Eivind had already made up his mind and Kathrine understood. Within a few weeks he had decided and the wedding was arranged. They were married on August 17, 1909. A few days later, they were on their way to Eidsvoll. Arrangements had been made for Eivind to continue his journalistic work to supplement the small income from teaching. Both were involved in teaching a whole variety of subjects: Kathrine taught Norwegian and arithmetic; Eivind, physics, chemistry, mechanics and later, history and psychology.

Whenever he could, Eivind accepted invitations to lecture. The Grundtvig ideal came into its own with him, as he became known in Denmark for his public lectures. "People are my field," he wrote to Kathrine. In June 1911, he was invited to give the keynote speech at a Danish National Conference in Hjørring. The speech was very well received and at the end of the conference they took this young Norwegian to their hearts. In a series of expressions of gratitude they spoke of him as an outstanding representative of the Norwegian people. Half-joking and half-boasting, he wrote home, "And now, everybody here thinks that I am a very important man, who is destined to become very famous."

The young schoolteacher had made his name in Denmark and also in Sweden. Consequently, he had a lecture tour at least once a year, either in Denmark or at the University of Lund in Sweden. But despite these lectures and his writing, he was faithful in his teaching and learned much from it. "These schoolchildren have opened up a new world to me," he wrote. Among the first items to master was the variety of the Norwegian language.

THE EDUCATOR

On the question of language Eivind met his first painful trial. "What form of Norwegian should be acceptable in the school?" This issue caused him trouble enough, but soon there were disputes over educational theories. He became personally involved when the controversy turned to "methods of teaching." He responded by outlining his own attitude. At first, he made the point very clearly that the aim of the Folk High School was now, as it had been from the beginning, to offer an all-round character-building education, awakening an interest in and directing attention to questions of lifestyle. He went on to explain that his task as teaacher was to help students in their search for worthwhile values in life.

In an article written in 1913, Berggrav gave an outline of his educational ideals. He used the Norwegian word *selvvirksomhet*, which means "making oneself" and implies the bringing out of potential in the personality of each individual. Principally, this consists of the belief that the person as a whole must be brought into the educational process: "Not only the understanding, but also the will, the heart and the body must develop, and the activity of the child should be related to the work of the community." Teaching was, for him, the mediation of a complete foundation for life by the personal inspiration of the teacher. "Enthusiasm and faith" must be communicated, he affirmed. "Without faith there is no action."

During his years at the Folk High School, these ideas were put into practice and modified by experience. Despite his many travels abroad and his frequent public lectures, his journalism and his articles on a full range of subjects, he put his heart into teaching for five years. Then, April 1914, he needed a change and went to Cambridge to continue his studies of religion and psychology. But he was not done with teaching! In the autumn, he returned to Norway as a replacement teacher at the Teacher Training College in Holmestrand.

Marriage and Family

Eivind and Kathrine enjoyed a good marriage. From the beginning Kathrine must have known what her role would be. While they were still students she had listened to him, comforted him in distress, and encouraged him in triumph. Eivind came to her as a son comes to a mother for comfort. But there was more than this. They began married life as partners with similar roles. The Folk High School demanded time, energy, and their talents and skills. They had equal shares in the day-to-day teaching and in the caring for the children. Eivind's frequent journeys meant that Kathrine had more than her share of the work. She rejoiced in his successes in Denmark and shared with him the problems of the school, not least the financial problems.

Their household responsibilities began to change, as is often the case, with the arrival of their first child. Otto was born on April 24, 1911. Care of the infant was Kathrine's, as she saw the need for Eivind to continue his traveling and lecturing. As a result, she was often alone with their firstborn. During 1911, Eivind held a six-week lecture tour in Northern Norway where he was deeply impressed by the people. That impression remained and he talked often with Kathrine about it. These long absences while the children were young caused some hardship on the family, which can be detected in the letters written by Kathrine. Yet there are no indications that Kathrine complained about the arrangements. She knew the man she had married and accepted him as he was, helping where she could to clear the path for his future.

After the birth of Otto, Eivind increased his study of psychology, especially child psychology. But he was seldom at home in 1911 when his son was growing and the child's bond with Kathrine was naturally always the stronger. The second child, Oivind Seip Berggrav was born August 4, 1914—an ominous date in European history. The third son, Jan, was born in 1923. Dag, the fourth and youngest son, was once asked to write about his family. He wrote, "My mother has five sons and one is called Daddy." Kathrine's role was a powerful one in the family, not only in her influence upon the sons, but also upon their father. In 1914 Eivind was still "growing up." The war that shook Europe from 1914 to 1918 required him to mature quickly as a husband, father, and man.

THE JOURNALIST

Much of Eivind Berggrav's journalistic writing was for the *Morgenblad,* but he became more and more interested in *Kirke og Kultur,* one of the premier periodicals in Denmark. Eivind's writing at this time was often cultural criticism. He later became editor of that journal, whose importance was recognized and grew under his editorship. Scandinavian editors gave the journal unanimous approval in those years of his editorship. Gunnar Engberg wrote glowingly: *"Kirke og Kultur* has become for Denmark the most important Scandinavian journal and its editor an extraordinarily gifted man."

Eivind had natural gifts for journalism and an easy and accessible style. In this period he developed a sensitive feel for the right expression. When he formed a particularly good phrase he rejoiced like a child! He was a master of words and striking combinations. The content of his articles and reports prove his ability to describe exactly the trends in modern social and cultural life, side by side with penetrating analysis. His success in public speaking flowed over into his writing.

When Berggrav became editor of *Kirke og Kultur,* he saw the journal as a bridge between the church and modern culture, spanning a self-evident abyss. At first, he laid the emphasis upon religion as the foundation of culture. This comes out markedly in the book reviews. His criticism of modern culture was that it allowed itself to be bound to the slogans of materialism, naturalism, and sensualism. He saw that positivism as a view of life had gone too far in the final decades of the 19th century. He challenged the uncritical admiration of scientific and technological progress. Putting forward an alternate view, he derived much of his thinking from the French philosopher Henri Bergson, who criticized intellectualism for its neglect in three specific areas: the inner life of a person, unmediated intuition, and the creative stream of life. Berggrav built upon this a strong case for a journalistic headline: "the mechanistic age is over, materialistic philosophy has failed."

In August 1913, Berggrav addressed a gathering of about 3,000 people in the vicinity of Tørring, Denmark, on the theme "Civilization Costs Money; Culture Costs Effort." The contrast was between two opposing views of the spiritual life. Culture was honorable because it embraced the cultivation of creative activity and ennobles what is given by nature. Bergson again, but also Rousseau! Civilization was a negative word, which carried with it a superficial and materialistic lifestyle, in which the cultural products became objects of a consumer society. There is no doubt that this is a great change from his youth, when he was fascinated, if not obsessed, with scientific developments and thought of himself as an engineer! His respect for tradition and inherited values led him to skepticism about many aspects of "modern life." He frequently attacked the view that modern technology and industrialization offer a solution to the world's problems.

The Political Commentator

Already as a student, Eivind was politically involved in the disputes over South Jutland and deplored the arrogance of the Prussians. But his real beginnings of political involvement came with the World War I and his discovery of the Ecumenical Movement.

He began as observer and commentator in Germany. His background tended to make him favorable to the German side. But the growth of Christian Socialism in England also attracted him. He had friends on both sides, which brought him into a very difficult situation as editor, commentator, and later war correspondent. In numerous articles he wrote of neutrality and partnership in relation to the warring states. The hardest problem for him was the political split among Christians; here the interests of the Ecumenical Movement came to the fore of his thinking.

In 1917, he was invited to an international conference of the churches in Uppsala, by Archbishop Nathan Söderblom, the Swedish ecumenical leader. Five non-belligerent countries were represented: Norway, Sweden, Denmark, Switzerland, and the Netherlands. The influence of this conference was considerable, particularly the resolutions that aimed at a comprehensive ecumenical program. For Berggrav the gathering was a significant event. As usual he attracted attention from observers and was singled out as one of the leading participants by the Swedish press. He interviewed well. The decisions of the conference spoke of the unity of the church, despite national and confessional divisions; they spoke of the task of the church to function as the conscience of the people, and to uphold the sanctity of law. With all this Berggrav was firmly in agreement. It helped him to clarify his own thoughts, particularly in his attitude to the war.

Writing often about the war from 1914 to 1919, Berggrav considered it his prime obligation to present a balanced report. The responsibility of the press was dear to him. He was critical of journalists, for example, when they expressed confident views of the conflict "based upon slender evidence." He was himself criticized for being "German-friendly." Undoubtedly his long and close relationship with Germany played a part. Berggrav was prepared to criticize the German power-politics he had witnessed in South Jutland, but he had a greater feel for German culture than for British or French or American social and cultural life. He thought that by involving himself in reconciliation and peace, rather than attacks on Germany, he could best achieve his purpose and help the northern countries to fulfill their historic role of building bridges into the future. To do this, his involvement, as well as that of neighboring nations, must be factual and not partisan. Scandinavia was neutral and he saw that as an honorable position, one that boded well for the future of Europe.

THE WAR CORRESPONDENT

In the course of his years, Eivind Berggrav had gathered much experience as journalist and reporter. But none of his previous assignments could compare with being sent to Germany in 1915 as war correspondent for *Morgenblad*. That summer he met two prominent figures: Friedrich Rittelmeyer, the anthroposophist preacher and founder of "The Christian Community" *(Christengemeinschaft)*, and Johannes Müller, an eloquent theologian. When Berggrav was in Nuremberg, his lodgings were near to a hall where Müller held forth to a spellbound audience for well over an hour on "Religious Renewal in Wartime." Berggrav himself wanted to study this subject during this short stay in Germany. But Müller's optimism left him a little skeptical regarding "renewal," which Berggrav saw as a kind of "August-religion," enthusiasm mixed with patriotism at the beginning of a war. Religion was Eivind's interest, but he wanted to know what was really happening when there appeared to be a revival. What was going on in the inner life of the individual? Psychological probing was part of Berggrav's journalistic skill. He wanted to discover the facts *accurately,* which meant looking behind the official façade and describing the personal aspect of the war. He was not satisfied with the way the press, in their dependence upon the wire services, handled the evidence often given for propaganda purposes. He believed that every statement must be studied from the inside out with the utmost care.

In August 1915, Berggrav had the opportunity to travel in Belgium and France, going to the Front. After that his writing about war was strongly influenced by his contact with the soldiers in the trenches. For them the greatest problem was the "bayonet war." Eivind quickly wrote a book, *The Soldier's Life and Religion,* perhaps the most important outcome of his travels. He focused on the question of "hand-to-hand fighting and Christianity," the title of one of its most original chapters. His descriptions show clearly his admiration for the soldiers who had experienced the tensions of trench warfare at the Front. He asserted that the kinds of strain, tension, and danger that these men faced "ennoble the soul and free it from weakness and indifference." Berggrav applied psychology in an attempt to discover how any person could endure the awful situation in the trenches when action started. He admired the soldiers who were compelled to remain in the trenches and experience the horrors of warfare. He saw many examples of the way in which ordinary soldiers confronted moral issues when they were required to inflict such pain and suffering on their fellow men. His observations led him to state that "war had brought the great issues of human life to the center of concern." The book was well-received with positive, even gushing reviews. It passed into three editions and was published also in Sweden, Finland, and Denmark.

Berggrav now saw, even more clearly, that the task of the journalist was to build bridges and put people on opposite sides of the barricades in touch with one another. Reconciliation by personal contact was what he now advocated as a means of understanding one another. The vocation of the journalist was not simply to report events, but also to analyze the fundamental motives and the hidden agenda. A description of actions alone was not enough; motives must be known.

The assignments in Germany afforded Berggrav a new strength in his journalistic skills. His articles began to show a sure grasp of the facts, but also a striking understanding of what was happening and what its consequences might be. He now ventured precise comment as well as analysis. As a result, he began to change both politically and theologically.

The Ultimate Decision

In 1915, Berggrav was still in a delicate phase of his spiritual life. He found himself defending liberal theologians and thereby criticizing the "old" school of theology dominant in Norway. His way back to faith had not been easy. He still had very serious doubts and secretly thought of himself as a "free-thinker." In this he was greatly helped by a young doctor, Kristen Andersen from Christiansand, who was able to remain a "free-thinker" within the church and keep his contacts and the trust of more traditional theologians.

Even before he went to Germany in 1915, he had received the sacraments. He was still uncertain about many of the claims of the Christian church, but his faith grew apace and, for all his doubts, the sacraments fed his spiritual growth. He surrendered at the altar. Many people expected great things of him. He heard from his teachers that he had leadership potential and a strong personality suited to youth work; many theologians expected great things from his studies of psychology. His academic work, however, did not bring forth the expected fruit. Despite his studies in Cambridge and the immense amount he had learnt in Germany, he was not yet ready to complete his qualifying thesis. With so many other alternatives, Berggrav turned again and again to the question of whether or not he should become a pastor.

Eivind had preached his first sermon at a university service in March 1915. During his lecture tours abroad he often preached in the cities and towns he visited. Yet, he did not feel himself competent to become a minister of religion. The fateful figure of his father emerged just in time. Otto Jensen was appointed Bishop of Hamar, and Eivind went to visit him and talk about his doubts and his latent faith. His father helped to clarify Eivind's belief in Christ as God's Son. But it was not the intellectual assurance that most affected him. On February 26, 1918, Otto Jensen died of a heart attack. In the months that followed, Eivind's thoughts turned around whether or not he could respond worthily to the life of his father. At first he had in mind publishing a memorial volume. He worked assiduously on this, seeking out the places where his father had grown up, reading most carefully the letters which over the years he had received from him, and compiling a volume that would show the stature of this man. It was all of no avail. He knew that he was avoiding the real decision. The question that would not go away was: "Why should I not try to become father's successor?"

HURDAL

In the autumn of 1919, Eivind accepted an invitation to become the pastor of Hurdal, a parish in the diocese of Akershus. The long journey back to faith and the agonizing question of his vocation ended, apparently in an obscure half-forgotten town in a rural area. To all appearances, the dream of great achievement lay in ruins. All his wide experience and his highly developed skills would now be given to his parish. He wrote a long personal letter to Kristen Andersen, after about six months in the parish, and noted, "Spiritually, I was already prepared for the ministry before I was invited or ordained." Later in that letter he added, "Father's death had changed everything." He now measured his life against that of his father: he too would be a minister.

Eivind did not stand alone in his work as pastor to his flock. His family began to play a much larger role in his life. Although he was soon caught up in traveling—the world had not forgotten this brilliant and persuasive lecturer—he discovered the real value of wife and children. Kathrine and the boys assumed a more important role in his work and career. In his lectures, Eivind frequently referred to marriage and to the education of children. Marriage, or perhaps Kathrine, had helped to form him as a whole person. The children too played their part. Their third son, Jan, was born in 1923 in Hurdal. By then, Otto was 12 and Oivind 10. The youngest child, Dag was born in 1925. The family was now complete. Years later (1949) when he gave a lecture to clergy wives, he made clear how important Kathrine had been for his work as pastor. She guaranteed him calm, he said, when enthusiasm and excitement gripped him. Her criticism of his manuscripts was often so strong that he called her his "wastepaper basket"! After her death, Eivind remarked of his beloved wife, "She was much concerned with people, sympathetic to others, but hard on herself."

For a time, Berggrav separated himself from Christiania. Its atmosphere and lifestyle became strange to him, he wrote in a letter. Life in Hurdal provided a sharp contrast from that in the town. This cultured pastor, who needed to remain in contact with theological and cultural ideas in the capital and at the same time integrate himself within the rural community which he served, must often have experienced powerful tensions. There was a great gap between Berggrav's modern version of theology and the tradition-bound Christian understanding of the people of Hurdal. But quite early Berggrav found a link between his own deep feeling for personal faith and experience and the simple faith of an unsophisticated people. He shared their love of God and their daily experience of sin and forgiveness. He shared their love of the Bible although he was well acquainted with biblical criticism. This personal and inward sense of faith in God came out in his sermons and his pastoral care. Despite theological and cultural differences, they knew that he shared their faith and, as their pastor, they knew they were locked in his heart. The people of the Inner Mission were at first suspicious of this "liberal" minister, but he strove to win them over. In this period of his life he nurtured a deep desire to be the pastor to *all* people in his parish, even those who could not share his theological position. More than most ministers he brought the pietistic groups into the life of the parish church. One motive in his preaching kept coming to the fore, both in Hurdal and in later life: his concern for the outsider, the bigot, the doubter, and the searcher. He was a good shepherd to everyone who lived in Hurdal.

3

Pastoral Work

Eivind Berggrav engaged in pastoral work for almost ten years (1919–28). The period was divided into two different kinds of care: pastor in the rural parish of Hurdal and chaplain in Oslo's new penitentiary.

One of the effects of Berggrav's work in Hurdal was to separate him from his former friends and other theologians in Oslo. He became critical of liberal theology, not so much intellectually as practically. As early as 1919, he surprised his friends by a review of a book by a well-known Swedish liberal theologian. Berggrav titled his review, "An Out-of-Date Book." He suggested that there was no place for constructive discussion in the book. "Liberal theology is no longer modern," he wrote. From 1920 onwards, Berggrav's attitude to the leading figures in the university faculty of theology was severely critical. His activities as pastor had given him a new perspective on theology. He saw that the liberal theologians had failed to make any useful contribution to parish work. But there was also a personal element in this alienation. Berggrav felt that he was not recognized by his one-time colleagues as a theologian and was no longer at home with them. It was quite different in Sweden. At the University of Lund he was recognized, trusted, respected and given opportunities.

Albert Schweitzer

Throughout his life, Berggrav retained a warm interest in foreign mission and the Ecumenical Movement. Whenever he met either in vigorous form, he was happy. In John R. Mott, he found a combination of world mission and ecumenical enthusiasm, which had won him over as a student. Now in Lund, Sweden, he met another man of equal stature. Berggrav had stayed longer than he had planned or needed for lectures and study in the Spring of 1922. Writing home to explain this delay, he said that he had met Albert Schweitzer, the Strasbourg theologian, at a lecture. He knew the name from his Marburg days, where Schweitzer was recognized as a famous exegete. At that time, he seemed to Berggrav to be as radical as one could be, but "warm hearted and very musical." Schweitzer had come to Lund to give an organ recital to raise money for his medical work in Lamberene in Africa. Now he seemed to Berggrav a bundle of energy and goodness. Within minutes they had become friends. The meeting with Schweitzer contributed greatly to his interest in missions. All his life he preserved a great respect for this extraordinary missionary.

The Ecumenical Movement

Berggrav had his first ecumenical experience during World War I. After the war, he showed considerable interest in the inter-confessional work of Archbishop Nathan Söderblom of Sweden, who involved him in work with the Lutherans of Hungary and Poland. But his most intense ecumenical experience came with the Stockholm Conference in August, 1925, made possible by Archbishop Nathan Söderblom. It was known as "The Universal Christian Conference on Life and Work" and dealt with a large number of contemporary questions, international, racial, social, and educational. Here the "Life and Work Movement" was born. Rome was not represented, but the Eastern Orthodox Churches were and over 600 delegates from 37 countries attended. Berggrav was admitted as part of the press corps. It was his first major contact with the world church in all its varieties.

Bishop Ammundsen of Denmark, whom Berggrav knew and admired for the way in which the Bishop reconciled Germans and Danes in his diocese, was present. Eivind also met George Bell, Dean of Canterbury, later Bishop of Chichester. Although the Germans sat in a solid block, still feeling isolated, Siegmund-Schulze and Deissmann played a major role in drafting the Message of the conference. In a long article, which he also published separately as an offprint, Berggrav described the conference as he saw it. He recognized it as a turning point of great significance in the whole history of the Ecumenical Movement. Although Berggrav was not an official representative, Söderblom arranged for him to meet the leading figures in the movement. There is no doubt of the friendship Berggrav had with Söderblom, who inspired him for the important role that he would play later in that movement.

THE PRISON CHAPLAIN

Berggrav learnt much in Hurdal, but his growing consciousness of ability to play a part at the national and international level led him to seek an appointment in Oslo. He was not clear about what kind of appointment he wanted, but it had to be in the capital. Towards the end of 1924, he was appointed prison chaplain to Oslo's new penitentiary. He quickly realized his lack of experience. He had little knowledge of prisons and no idea how to deal with prisoners. But he would be in the capital and he could learn. In a short time, Berggrav acquired a clear and confident view of his work, both within the institution and outside. It was during his five years as prison chaplain that he took over the editorship of *Kirke og Kultur* and many of his best articles appeared in this journal. The Stockholm Conference influenced many of his early articles on the Ecumenical Movement, but soon other articles appeared on the politics of prisons and prisoners. Eivind did not hide his sympathy with those who pressed for prison reform; he even played his part in it, introducing new principles in dealing with prisoners and describing his methods and philosophy in his writings.

For Berggrav, the penitentiary was an educational establishment with the goal of helping prisoners return to life in the community. He arranged for well-known people to visit the prison and talk to and with the prisoners, giving them an insight into life "on the outside." At that time he was very interested in trying to discover all he could about leading personalities. He felt that the prisoners might find in them valuable role models. One of his great achievements was to persuade the polar explorer, Roald Amundsen, to visit and make a presentation. Earlier, Berggrav had written an article about Amundsen's homecoming in 1906 with great enthusiasm. It was therefore a highpoint in his program of visitors when, on June 13, 1925, Roald Amundsen visited the prison and spoke in the chapel for three-quarters of an hour on his exploration of the polar region. The prisoners were thrilled. Later, Berggrav invited many other achievers like Captain Ruser-Larsen and the aviator Bernt Balchen. The purpose of these visits was to provide positive models and to encourage character development.

PSYCHOLOGY AND RELIGION

As prison chaplain, Berggrav had ample opportunities to assess human life at its extreme. He knew enough psychology to make a serious study of about 1200 men, with whom he was in regular contact over long periods of time. Before he left the prison service, he published the results of these observations in a book entitled *The Soul of a Prisoner—and Our Own* in the autumn of 1928. His purpose was to describe the influence of the prison's atmosphere on the state of mind of the prisoner. Once he had left the prison service, he saw that his observations on this theme applied much more universally than he had supposed. There is nothing unique about the influence of the prison atmosphere—everyone is affected by the milieu in which he or she lives and the effect can be measured.

Berggrav had changed over these ten years. Pastoral work in two such different conditions of life as Hurdal and the Oslo penitentiary had taught him much. It was a powerful leap from the rural life and deliberate speech of the farmers of Hurdal to the prison inmates of Oslo. Certainly his prison service gave him insights into worlds, which until then, he had known only from the outside. It broadened both his religious and human horizons. Berggrav found himself and his calling. He was, of course, much more mature and more confident. He knew now that he could not give up his faith. He struggled with doubts from time to time, but his faith was more balanced and this showed in his preaching as well as his writing.

A Danish journalist who met Berggrav in 1928 in Copenhagen was impressed by his confident manner and the ease with which he related to young people. "There was nothing of the 'minister' about him," he said, "he was curt and terse, energetically determined and quick, as though one had to do with a successful businessman." That is not entirely a flattering portrait, but it confirms in part the reason why Berggrav was so popular—his lack of clerical airs and his ability to relate to people at all social levels. In the early days at Hurdal, he had had difficulties partly due to his own uncertainties and his unfulfilled ambitions.

In 1927, looking back on five years in Hurdal and four as prison chaplain, he tried to assess the role of a pastor and examine himself as to whether he had lived up to his ideals. In rough summary, this is what he wrote: "A minister has to represent both the human and the divine. The people expect from their minister an authority, which is timeless and valid. At the same time they want their pastor to be like themselves, or rather what they think they should be. He must live up to it even when they do not. They look for humanity in him, but the minister must lead them beyond humanity." That, in short, was the quintessence of Berggrav's ideal of the pastor. He had not always lived up to it, but he never forgot it.

Shortly after leaving Hurdal, Eivind presented his dissertation to the university at Christiania on October 25, 1925. *The Invasion of the Human Life of the Soul by Religion* was published in Norwegian shortly afterward and in 1929 a German translation appeared. It was well-received and praised even in Norway. The most favorable reviews came from Germany. In a German periodical, Pastor Hermann Günther wrote in superlative terms of Berggrav's elegant argument, perceptive style, showing the incomparable quality and scientific knowledge of the author.

RELIGION BEYOND THE BOUNDARIES

The dissertation was original in its application to religion. Eivind was not the first to see the human spirit as restless and always probing the limits. He knew this himself in his childhood, as he searched beyond the waterfall. Critics of his dissertation usually pointed out that he was prone to go beyond his subject. But his thesis was that the natural human restlessness, which searches out beyond the boundaries, leads to religion. "Without boundaries, man becomes paralyzed by a vague feeling of endlessness; without stepping over the boundary, human life becomes fossilized and the person loses the power which drives him into new understandings." This, he points out, is to grow morally and make cultural development possible. Berggrav's main contribution was that the tendency to step over the boundaries culminates in religion. Such a venture might be construed as trying to prove the truth of religion or the existence of God from psychology. Some critics interpreted his thesis in this manner. But this was not Berggrav's purpose. In plain words, he said, "Neither God nor the relationship with God can be deduced from psychology."

Most people saw great promise in this dissertation, but they usually tried to recruit him for their own causes. He saw this danger with Rudolf Otto quite early. What few recognized at first was that Berggrav was blending two powerful influences—liberal theology and the pietism of experience. He was captive to neither.

PERSONAL EMANCIPATION: JOHANNES MÜLLER AND SCHLOSS ELMAU

Berggrav's academic work was not finished in Lund, but in a quite different place. In the winter of 1922, he and Kathrine took a holiday at Schloss Elmau in the beautiful surroundings of the Bavarian Alps. It was owned by Johannes Müller, the eloquent theologian who had impressed him in Nuremburg in 1915. Müller had used Schloss Elmau for many years to encourage mental health and a positive attitude to life. Many who went there suffered from depression or the strain of fundamentalist piety. As early as 1898, Müller had published a journal, *For the Healing of Personal Life*. It was widely read and much discussed. It became known later as the "Green Pages." Inevitably it interested Berggrav. Muller published several books at the turn of the century on the theme of personal emancipation. Then in 1916, he founded an academy, which had as its objective to be a refuge from the strains of theological and ethical controversies and for those who needed to develop their own personal life. Eivind and Kathrine went for a holiday to relax from the strain of disputes about the school in 1922. It had been a difficult year at the Folk High School in Eidsvoll; Kathrine saw the need to get away and Eivind chose the place. The vacation later proved to be very significant for Berggrav's emancipation. They stayed five weeks and Berggrav was greatly improved in health. He took long walks with Müller and began to understand the value of what Schloss Elmau was doing for pastors who were confused by the controversies in which they had reluctantly been involved. He wrote to a friend that he had learnt nothing new, but rather was confirmed in what he had experienced over the past ten or fifteen years. He could still criticize Müller, as he had done in 1915, and he certainly disagreed when Müller entirely rejected the conventional expressions of Christianity and the traditions of the church. But Müller's personality and his attitude to life—especially in the relaxed atmosphere of Schloss Elmau and the Bavarian Alps—fascinated him and he was determined to come back. He returned, two years later, this time alone. His purpose on this return was to gather strength to complete his dissertation. Müller shared with Eivind his attitude to life, which was wider than intellectual, embracing all facets of human life. This time Eivind "learned" that it was not enough to do one's duty in life; in retrospect, one should also enjoy it. He began to understand his own depressions or what he called "nervousness." "Enjoy it" became a part of his philosophy. Those who worked and traveled with Berggrav in later years affirmed that he never departed from that lesson.

Between the two visits, he published in 1923 an article in *Kirke og Kultur* on Müller's program. In that article he described his Socratic gift for bringing out the spiritual possibilities of life that were locked within the individual, helping him to unfold. His ideal was the free, simple and natural life, which liberates one from the pressure of systems and the rigidity of imposed forms.

On that second visit in 1924, Berggrav wrote in one of his regular letters to Kathrine that Müller had two ways of influencing people: he was either very critical and even subversive, arousing strong opposition, or he gave free rein to his own inner feelings, offering something of himself to the listener and moving him to a sense of confidence. Of the first method, Berggrav said, the feeling of opposition to Müller's exaggerated statements opened the way for Müller to "plough his acre." Of the second, Berggrav commented, "Müller is like the sun and soft rain which sets us free to grow." During the 1924 visit, Berggrav experienced both sides of Müller. He saw through his methods and tried to disentangle himself from the trap, but he failed and Müller left him shattered. To Kathrine, he wrote,

"Despite all, I really had the feeling of being set free from the greatest burden of my life." Now he began to understand the burden that he had unsuspectingly carried on his back. He needed help beyond what Müller could give.

Psychoanalysis

Inevitably Eivind turned to psychoanalysis, despite his suspicion of the practice. He recognized what his problems were: his intense interest in his father, his crisis over the relationship between the rational and the irrational, and the sense that there was something deep within his psyche which he had not yet faced. All this, given the primitive state of counseling at the time, meant, psychoanalysis.

His encounters with psychoanalysis to this point in his life did not encourage him. In his dissertation there is no mention of it or apparent influence on his thinking. Both in theory and in practice Berggrav had serious reservations. He suspected that in psychoanalysis one had to do with a strict world view, a new morality and perhaps even a new religion. He was also critical of those who saw psychoanalysis as a means of renewal in the church's pastoral work. For years he contested the view that one or another of the schools of psychology— Freud, Jung, or Adler—was superior to the traditional pastoral care of the church. This was most clearly expressed in an article written as late as 1932, "Can Psychology Kill?" It was his view that pastoral work influenced by new psychology would lose the ability to react spontaneously and fail to see the humanity in people. Again in 1932 he wrote to a radical theologian who was deeply involved in psychoanalysis that he, Berggrav, would never submit to analysis! He explained that he feared the effect would be to make him egocentric. But, despite this reservation, Berggrav went to Switzerland in 1933 to see the Freudian analyst and Protestant pastor, Oscar Pfister.

For some time, Berggrav had suffered from a prolonged depression. He thought a study period and a long stay at

Schloss Elmau would help. Then a Danish friend suggested that he should undergo analysis with Pfister, not only for professional growth, but for personal reasons. Johannes Müller had often advised the same. Whatever reservations he might have about Freud, whose attitude to religion was clearly negative, he could not have the same troubles with the Reverend Oscar Pfister, a respected Protestant minister. But he kept his reasons for the visit secret from all except Kathrine. Officially he said that he was going to Switzerland to study analytical psychology under Carl Gustav Jung. He left at the beginning of February 1933, just as Hitler came to power in Germany.

In regular letters to Kathrine, Eivind described his experiences. Oscar Pfister often asked him to describe his dreams; in daily analysis they discussed their meaning. After his third session, Eivind wrote, "I can see very well that this will take three weeks, or perhaps even longer." While there he thought he could prepare a series of lectures, which he was due to give later in Sweden, on the relation between soul and body. The analysis demanded all his energy, but it also stimulated his mind, and he could write to Kathrine, "Never have I been so relaxed, while at the same time, productive in my work. I can write for hours without getting tired. Often I can compose something for my lecture without getting into the usual sweat." But this was no peaceful retreat. The days in Zürich were hectic. Pressure came from outside. In Norway there was intense discussion about the American play, *Green Pastures*; Berggrav had been involved in the debate. There came also the question whether he would be prepared to become the Minister of Religion and Education in Mowinckel's Foreign Office. When he told Pfister of this invitation from the Foreign Office, Pfister at once replied that Eivind could be ready to become the government Minister within two weeks if he could be rid of his hyper-activity and the melancholy reactions it imposed. Berggrav was himself far more skeptical. On February 13, 1933, he could not bring himself to write his daily letter to Kathrine, but in the next day's letter he explained. He was becoming dissatisfied with Pfister. At first, he thought Pfister far too hurried; he also disagreed with his search for a childhood complex, which Pfister thought that he had repressed. There followed an ambivalent relationship. Suddenly the analysis session began to yield something. On the day after when he could write to Kathrine he said that "never had the sessions yielded so much!" The complex from childhood had proved superficial. All he could say at that point was that "there is something quite other emerging than what Pfister had at first suspected." Perhaps his relation to his father had been exposed. Pfister expressed the opinion that his father was his "figure of destiny."

Over the next weeks, he saw Pfister less often in his office, though they took to walking sessions, much as he had done with Johannes Müller. Berggrav found these less satisfactory and he began to seek out other influences in Zürich—Emil Brunner and Carl Gustav Jung. On 21st February, he contacted Jung.

CARL GUSTAV JUNG

There were many reasons why Jung was more congenial to Berggrav's interests. Pfister had used Freudian psychology to help his pastoral work—to Freud's surprise that a "godless Jew" could help a Christian minister. Jung had broken with Freud after four or five years of intense cooperation. Freud had insisted that others accept his sexuality theory like a dogma. Freud had also refused to recognize the existence of supernatural phenomena. Jung saw the importance of sexuality, but wished to understand it more profoundly than its personal significance or its biological function. Jung sought its "spiritual aspect and its numinous meaning." This left him open to spiritual causes of neurosis as well as health of mind.

When Berggrav contacted Jung there was an immediate response and they met next day (February 22, 1933). Berggrav was entranced. "I felt free and happy," he wrote. "With Pfister it was always heavy and I was unsure of myself. Not so with Jung. He worked in a rounded way, powerful, confident, and manly. I believe Jung will be a rich source for the future of psychology. He is way ahead of his time." Both personally and professionally, Jung left an indelible impression upon Berggrav. Berggrav had read some of Jung's writings before he met him and it was not long before those writings came alive and greatly influenced his own writing.

Jung very strongly influenced Berggrav's next publication, *Body and Soul in Personal and Spiritual Life* (Oslo, 1933). In this book he entered into a whole series of questions that had not concerned him until then. His explanation in the Foreword was that he intended to contribute to the understanding of how Christians could discover the body. Jung's analytical psychology had made it possible for Berggrav to establish that apart from physical experiences in the body, the psyche had access to other forces, scientifically explained as "the unconscious."

Before the publication of the book, Berggrav used similar material in his lectures given at the University of Uppsala. Swedish author Sven Stolpe recorded his impression of those Uppsala lectures in the spring of 1933:

> The university hall was crowded and I cannot remember a time when a lecturer has held the attention of such a crowd by the content of what he offered in his lectures. The hall was deadly silent, gripped by the profound thought, captivated by the brilliance of new formulations, filled with hope by the view that was opened up before them and happy to be sitting at the feet of such a lecturer. Time and again, he raised a smile, because this Norwegian told everyday anecdotes and allowed his irony full course. Whoever heard these lectures could never forget them. Here rich artistry appeared in a genial personality in the full bloom of youth. Leaving the hall, one felt one's intellectual and spiritual life raised and renewed in a very extraordinary way.

In his lectures, Berggrav made the clear connection between bodily and spiritual functions and the ordinary experiences of life. In the book, however, he also elaborated on his earlier ideas expressed in the phrase "stepping over the boundaries." His work was enriched by depth psychology. Jung's writings and insights helped Berggrav to posit an independent spiritual reality. But the gap between Jung's psychology and theology was a great deal more difficult to span than Berggrav had at first thought. The determination to emphasize the religious worth of Jung's psychology led Berggrav to give a rather vague definition of "the spiritual." It took him too far in the direction of religious irrationalism.

RELIGIOUS EMOTIONS IN THE LIFE OF A HEALTHY PERSON

Some years before meeting Jung, Berggrav had written about emotional feelings in religion. The book published in Oslo in 1927 bore the title, *Religious Emotions in the Life of a Healthy Person*. Berggrav had in mind ordinary, healthy Christians and the kind of emotional disturbances that occur in the normal course of their religious life. His work was well-received by all sections of the religious community in Norway. This was an early sign of his ability to reconcile conflicting and often belligerent divisions in the church. The conservatives praised him for his loyalty to Luther and his respectful quotations. His interest in questions about the emotions had clear affinities with the concerns of those within pietistic circles. Berggrav wrote about religious experience and was classified as an experiential theologian.

At the same time he warned against over-emphasizing the role of the emotions. He was clear about the danger of treating emotional experiences in isolation. It was important for him that they should always be related to functions of the mind and of the will. Emotional experience cut off from the functioning of the mind, as in mysticism and emotional religiosity, gives rise to two related consequences: Religion becomes amoral and infused with emotional vagueness or it runs the danger of producing an irreligious ethic, a rigid moralism, which destroys the connection between religious experience and responsible moral behavior. Emotional experience and mystical ecstasy require the guidance of Christian ethics.

KARL BARTH

The Swiss theologian Karl Barth was becoming one of the most influential theologians in the Protestant world. Slightly younger than Berggrav, Barth attracted many clergy and laypersons as followers and dominated the churchmen of his own generation. He became particularly important during the Nazi period and provided the basis for a theological resistance in Germany to those who allowed Nazi doctrines to penetrate the thinking and activities of the churches. His influence was not as strong in Norway as it was in Germany and the Netherlands. Barth was not a Lutheran, but stood squarely in the Reformed tradition. His followers ridiculed Berggrav's efforts to link psychology to theology. From their point of view, there was no point in talking about examining the soul to discover anything to do with religion. Instead, one should direct his gaze towards God's dealing with man. In this new, "dialectic theology," the psychology of religion was ignored or discounted. Berggrav wrote an article for *Kirke og Kultur* entitled "The Study of the Mind and Theology." In this piece he surveyed the development of psychology over the past 30 years and related his conclusions to Barth's theology. The two men were very different, although both had the power to reconcile differing traditions within the church. Berggrav was inclined to listen to other views and understand them; Barth usually had a much harsher judgment upon those with whom he disagreed.

A PROFESSIONAL CAREER

While Berggrav was prison chaplain in Oslo, there were strong hints that he might be appointed to a secure academic post in the Theological Faculty of the University of Oslo. Consequently, over the next few years he agreed to give lectures in the Faculty on Systematic Theology and the Psychology of Religion. In addition to his work as chaplain he also taught a Seminar in Practical Theology. His expertise in the field of the Psychology of Religion was widely recognized in the academic world. His dissertation appeared in Germany in 1929 and was reviewed in a number of academic journals. About the same time he received an honorary doctorate from the University of Kiel. There were others who recognized that Berggrav could have made a major contribution as a full-time faculty member at the University of Oslo. But nothing came of the lectures and he did not obtain a permanent place in the Theological Faculty. Once he expressed his bitter disappointment to his counselor, Johannes Müller, that the faculty had blocked his way. But he decided that his career would not be in the Academy; he would serve God and the world in the church.

4

The Norwegian Bishop
of the Arctic

In 1928, Berggrav was nominated as a candidate for the Bishopric of Hålogaland, the most northern diocese of Norway. He was not yet 44, and as a result many references were made to his youth before and after his appointment. Eivind, too, was aware of his tender age—not only was he younger than the other bishops, but he also questioned his ongoing doubts about his faith and his own lack of pastoral experience.

That he was nominated for the office was no surprise to those who knew him. He was reckoned among the most active pastors, full of initiative and competent in many fields, not least in practical theology. In the eyes of some, however, a far more serious issue was his past association with liberal theologians. The old church controversies were not at an end and the confrontation between Liberals and Conservatives was as strong as ever. Faced with this situation, Berggrav wrote some articles in *Kirke og Kultur* that not only attempted to address the situation but marked a milestone in his own theological and ecclesiastical development. In one article, "Contemporary Theology," he separated himself from the Liberals and stated that liberal theology was a kind of "Christian reductionism." At the same time he aligned himself with a positive, constructive theology and made no secret of his sympathy with the "personal Christianity" of the Pietists. The article made it more difficult to place him in the theological landscape.

Another important article, written in the winter of 1928, concerned the controversial case of the radical theologian Kristian Schjelderup. The Minister of Religion and Education had refused to sanction the candidacy of this very liberal theologian, nominated for the post of regional minister. The action of the Minister of Religion and Education caused great concern among liberal theologians and some declared that his action as Minister was invalid.

Berggrav supported the action of the Minister in this matter; he denounced the system and declared that the church had failed to recognize its own responsibility. The article, "At the Church Door," maintained that Schjelderup should never have been admitted as a pastor with such a theological record. But the main theme of his article was to clarify Berggrav's view of the church: "According to our Church Order, the keeper of the door of the church is the Bishop, not the Minister of Religion and Education." While many were trying to modernize the church by making it more democratic, Berggrav launched a different program. "The church needs a stronger standing for the Bishops." They should be the mouthpiece of the church, he argued, and responsible for its appointments. "Before we can find the right word to the world, we must be in the position of pressing for a truly episcopal authority."

Despite his repeated criticism of liberal theology, he was still regarded as the candidate for this faction, even though he was probably "conservative" from the point of view of many Liberals. During the election it was generally assumed that he stood outside the "Parties." The result of the election for the Bishopric of Hålogaland left Berggrav in third place, but he was nevertheless appointed by the Minister.

HÅLOGALAND

The northern diocese of Hålogaland is like no place else in Norway. It lies on the map like the frayed edges of a torn cloth. Finland and Sweden seem to be pushing it into the sea. Instead of the browns and greens of the southern part of Norway, its landscape is of a rich warm shade of gray. The mountains are lower, but sharper in form and fiercer in mood. Hundreds of remote wild fjords, narrow sounds, and storm-swept islands create a beautiful coast. When Berggrav arrived in Tromsø, at that time the capital of the diocese and the seat of the Bishop, he wrote to his friend, the Swedish Archbishop Nathan Söderblom: "Here it is stormy, dark, and cold, but the people are bright, easygoing, and warm-hearted. I think I am going to like it here." A few months later, writing to another Swedish friend: "Summer seems to make an endless journey. It dominates vast horizons. The Norwegian coast is 360 (Norwegian) miles, of which I alone have to care for 206!" Until the diocese was divided in 1952, it included all three northern provinces: Troms, Finnmark, and Nordland.

On a map with the North Pole at its center, this extensive diocese looks like a crescent, bulging out towards the Pole. North Cape is the most northerly point in Europe. Apart from the long border with Finland and with Sweden, it also extends to a short border with Siberia, no more than 20 Norwegian miles from Murmansk. In the nineteenth century, Norway and Tsarist Russia both asserted their rights to the island *Novaya Zemly*. It too would have been part of Berggrav's diocese if the Russians had not moved many *Nenets* from the Urals to live there in the 1870s to claim the island. As it was, the new bishop of Hålogaland rubbed shoulders with the Soviet Union at the extreme point of his diocese.

The USSR took its borders seriously. At the frontier with Norway, a Soviet border notice proclaimed, "This territory is *sacred* to the USSR." Berggrav frequently remarked that he liked the thought of an atheistic regime using a religious word to protect its territory!

Travel in this region of Norway was never easy. The distances and climate imposed a great strain upon Berggrav in his desire to visit his vast—or rather long—diocese. The diocese was not only extensive, but also diverse—ethnically, socially, and culturally. Religious life was not as uniform as in most of Norway. These realities presented the new Bishop with genuine challenges in his ministry.

INITIAL DIFFICULTIES

The seat of the Bishop was in Tromsø, from which Eivind Berggrav resolved to visit his scattered parishes. It was important for him to know his parish priests and their congregations. But transportation in his diocese was difficult. Much of it had to be done by sea in stormy weather and Berggrav was never a good sailor. Even more difficult were the journeys inland where some of his parishes lay. In Finnmark the only means of travel was by reindeer. Berggrav's dramatic description of such a journey in March 1936 became one of his most popular talks throughout Scandinavia.

Transportion was not his only problem. Many of the parishioners in his congregations did not understand Norwegian. The Lapps had their own language, which he could not understand; neither could they understand him. This was accentuated in Finnmark by desperate poverty. Although poverty was endemic throughout Norway, it was particularly bad in Finnmark. Infant mortality was double that of the rest of the country, hygiene was terrible, poverty and hunger were widespread. It was worst among Lapps, particularly those roaming the coastal areas. Berggrav suffered much from the language barrier. His usual friendly talks and easy contacts one-to-one were no longer possible. For some years, Finnmark was like a foreign country to him. Eventually this negative attitude to Finnmark changed. He learned to respect the singular Lapp culture and maintained that the Lapps had the right "to be different." This was not the usual attitude at that time. Most Norwegians wanted to integrate the Lapps into the "superior" Norwegian culture. Berggrav was ahead of his time.

THE LAPPS

No less than a dozen different Arctic peoples encircle the North Pole, north of the tree line (or Arctic Circle). Berggrav's diocese encompassed a considerable part of Lapland with its unofficial capital in Kautokeino. For centuries these people had lived in dependence upon reindeer. In earlier days, the animals were hunted wild and tamed only to pull sledges. In the 16th and 17th centuries, gun-bearing hunters reduced the population. The Lapps bred and domesticated their own stocks, but the reindeer remained near wild, an essential quality for the annual migration. They spent the summer south of the tree line, where the crust of snow was thin and the reindeer could find pasture. If there was a heavy crust or deep snow, which was rare in the near-desert Arctic, it spelt disaster for man and beast. This precarious existence required a tightly controlled mode of life, in which every movement was a ritual for survival.

THE LAESTADIANS IN NORWAY

The Lapps were the last people in Europe to be evangelized. In 1844, Lars Levi Laestadius, a priest in Karasuando in Northern Sweden, gave up his parish and began to seek new life for the Christian community by forming groups of men and women anticipating a revival of true religion. The first community was formed on December 5, 1845, when revival broke out. Rumor spread and the official church regarded the "Laestadians" unfavorably. Some three months after the formation of the first community in Karasuando, the movement spread to Norway—seven miles, across the Swedish border, to

Kautokeino. The earnest preaching of Laestadius and his followers persuaded the Lapps in one village after another.

Berggrav studied this evangelical, revival movement which was still alive in his day. Its characteristics were devotion to Luther and long—all-day—worship services. They adhered to a strict code of conduct, which extended to the manner of dress and the language. The movement spread rapidly in the 1840s from Kautokeino in West Finnmark to Lyngen in North Troms and Ibestad in South Troms, bordering on Ofoten in Nordland.

By the time Berggrav became Bishop, the movement was spread throughout his diocese. It was still regarded somewhat unfavorably by most of the official churchmen, but Berggrav showed a kindly interest in this intense movement, particularly among the Lapps. He retained that interest and, in 1956, insisted that a study of the use of the Bible in the living situation of the churches, a project sponsored by the United Bible Societies, should include how the Laestadians used the Bible. The study demonstrated how closely they kept to Luther's Bible, using a translation into their language of an eighteenth-century German edition, presumably the version that Laestadius used. They spent all day in church on Sunday, eating their meals and feeding their babies at the congregational building. During the day there were extensive readings of Luther's Sermons. They had been isolated from most European influence, but already in 1956, they were worried about their young people who were showing signs of attraction to the tourist ships, which brought modern western ideas into their waters. In Berggrav's time that had not yet happened. They were a godly people and Berggrav respected them. In his 1937 book *Spenningens Land: Visitas-glimt fra Nord-Norge* (*Land of Tensions: Glimpses of Unknown Norway*), Beggrav explored the faith and life of the Laestadians. A better title, given his portrayal, might have been *Land of Contrasts*. Norway was truly a diverse place. Berggrav also made reference in this work to the semi-nomads from Finland who began to migrate in the 1920s, establishing villages in parts of North Troms and Finnmark, a people called Kvenen.

THE FINNISH THREAT

At the time of the migration of the Kvenen, a political conflict in the Arctic Circle was developing. In Finland, a nationalistic group was interested in the Kvenish minority in Norway. On the Norwegian side, people spoke of the "Finnish Threat." These views threatened the relationship between the two nations.

In his pastoral wisdom, Eivind Berggrav remained silent on the issue. A letter written by Berggrav to the Norwegian Foreign Minister on November 30, 1929, makes his position clear on the subject of Finland and the Kvenish population of North Norway. The letter was titled "Our Psychological Relationship with Finland." This was the key for Berggrav. He saw the conflict between Norway and Finland as psychological, rather than political. Finland attracted the Kvenen and Lapps, who looked upon the neighboring country to the east—Norway—as hostile. Berggrav proposed that measures be taken to help assimilate the Kvenen and Lapps to their home in Norway—building churches for the Kvenen, finding more interpreters and improving the knowledge of Lappish and Finnish among the pastors. At the same time a modification of the traditional Norwegian way of teaching politics in schools was necessary. According to Berggrav, the hard-line stand previously taken against the Finnish action had brought the Norwegians nowhere. A more moderate policy towards language and culture, he suggested, could bring the Lapps closer to the Norwegian population. This policy proposed by Berggrav found wide support, and a series of chapels were built along the border.

Outwardly, it was not at all apparent what role the Bishop played in the Finland question. It is now clear from documents (not in the episcopal archives, but elsewhere) that Berggrav did play a key role in diffusing "the Finnish threat." He was the principal supervisor and protector of the various efforts to bring and maintain peace. His initial plan for a political and cultural strategy, which meant his work as supervisor and controller of Norwegian-Finnish contacts in the cultural and religious field, were successful. He worked particularly closely with the Head of the General Staff of the Army, Colonel Otto Ruge, and the civilian governor of Finnmark, Hans Gabrielsen. These three controlled the Press Service for Finland, which had as its objective to keep the Kvenen constantly in view, and to know when the Finnish visitors were approaching.

Was Berggrav's main consideration in this matter religious or political? He kept his activities fairly secret; perhaps because his own conviction was that the church should confine itself to religious matters. It is difficult to believe, however, that his only motive was religious, although in many ways, such as the building of churches along the border, he benefited the church. In truth, Berggrav had entered the political arena. His actions are the first link to his involvement and work, in the winter of 1939/1940, as diplomat and peacemaker, as well as in his activities during the occupation of Norway by the Germans.

VISITING THE CONGREGATIONS

The churches of North Norway were quick to note that Bishop Berggrav had new and unconventional ways of getting in contact with the congregational life. Newspaper reports of his episcopal visitations comment mostly on his naturalness, free from episcopal pomp and clerical language. One article, reporting his visit to Varda, noted that his familiarity in no way detracted from his episcopal authority. Berggrav could be sharp and unsparing in his criticism when he disapproved of relationships in the congregations. His judgment of a congregation was not only based upon first impressions of a visit or what he heard from the church council. He was also dependent upon personal contacts with those listeners, whose comments he felt were reliable.

Berggrav's own letters about these visitations give us an insight into his changing moods after meeting with the congregations. One day he would express only failure, but on the next day, he felt pleased at how "good" the Service was. Berggrav made high demands upon himself; after long periods of visitations and writing, he was often exhausted. In the spring of 1931, Kathrine wrote to her friend, Magda Smith, that Eivind was irritable and depressed, and at times she feared he would have a nervous breakdown. She also thought that she knew the cause: "I believe he is beset with the idea that he is inadequate for the position he holds; quite simply, he has an inferiority complex. You would hardly believe that when he is in a good mood." Perhaps the changing moods came from the experiences he had when he was living in Lund and Eidsvoll. The effects of that time had never quite left him. Berggrav's ideal was to be a "pure instrument" for God's use. He was clear about his own tendencies—to be domineering and wanting always to be in the center of activities. A journalist on the staff of a Tromsø newspaper once wrote a caricature of Berggrav. The Bishop was disturbed, not because it was untrue, but because he recognized himself in it! Writing to Kristen Andersen in the spring of 1933, Kathrine explained that somewhere in his unconscious lay a desire to be admired and a compulsion to be a perfect Berggrav. This, she said, he admitted in a very self-critical moment.

UNDERSTANDING THE CLERGY

A few years after he became Bishop of Hålogaland, Berggrav held a series of lectures with the clergy of his diocese. He spoke about the value of their ministry and the contributions that contemporary thought, including psychology, could make to their work. In his discussions he learned a great deal about the problems and conflicts encountered by the pastors, especially in their relations with one another. He discerned their tendency to compare themselves and their progress with the others and noted the jealousy that often followed these comparisons. There was nothing surprising about the situation, but Berggrav detected among these pastors five distinctive attitudes that gave rise to conflict and pain: the urge to improve one's position; feelings of inferiority; feelings of being unjustly dealt with; a combative reaction; the instinct to withdraw in disapproval. He recognized these responses as common to all communities—even when they are dressed-up in clerical attire or explained as religious principles! Yet with confidential counseling and confession such problems could be handled. During the 1930s, many of the clergy in Scandinavia were strongly influenced by the "Oxford Group," a religious movement based in England that emphasized personal sharing and guidance among believers. Norwegian pastors were, therefore, prepared for the Bishop's teaching about confession and repentance.

Berggrav's ambition was to be a pastor to his clergy. In many of his letters the Bishop gave pastoral advice and support to his clergy, whether it concerned relations with the local church or family and marital problems. There were also many letters of thanks from the clergy to their Bishop for a personal talk or a helpful letter. Berggrav was deeply appreciated within the diocese.

Yet a small minority was not satisfied with him and worked systematically against him. The great majority, however, looked upon him as a superior authority that gave them great security. The Bishop certainly treated his "favorites" better than others. When he thought that he had to deal with a pastors—for idleness, incompetence, or failure—he could be very stern, at times almost shockingly hard. He set high standards for himself, but also for his clergy.

A BENJAMIN AMONG THE BISHOPS

The bishops had a young, energetic man in their midst and they soon detected that he had a great talent with his pen.

In this he was a master. For the first time, the bishops had a journalist among them, and the public soon recognized this as well. He was adept in searching out the details and bringing them together in a clear, meaningful statement. During the 1930s, the Bishops' Conference had developed in an uncontrolled way, allowing inconsequential discussion of minutiae and vague, general issues. Berggrav played a key role in defining a formal status for the Bishops' Conference as part of the constitution of the church. This was vital for the drive towards recognizing the authority of the College of Bishops.

The standing that Berggrav acquired step-by-step in the Bishops' Conference could have led to the impression some had that he was domineering. He was well aware of this himself. In 1936, he wrote that it no longer gave him pleasure to be so domineering, although he quickly added "at least I think so." He thought he still dominated, but he modified his tone. This was evident when the issue was the important question of the ordination of women, which he had personally put on the agenda for discussion.

DISPUTE WITH THE MINISTRY OF RELIGION AND EDUCATION

Dealing with these concerns at the Bishops' Conference was only one example of the disputes between the authority of the Bishops and the Ministry of Religion and Education. Once, the Minister of Religion and Education called Berggrav into his office to have a serious word with him. For several days there was a tense relationship between the Bishops and the Head of the Ministry. This tug-of-war between the two authorities had its origin in the similar problem that Berggrav had already in 1928 with the Schjelderup affair. After that, throughout the early thirties, Berggrav worked intensively on a Constitution for the church.

Among other developments, he was critical of the proposal to appoint a Church Adviser as the highest authority in the church. Such an appointment, he saw, would undermine the proper authority of the bishops. He did not share the view that church democratization would lead to emancipation of the church, but feared that it would lead to secular authorities imposing their views upon the church, undermining the proper authority of the Bishops' Conference.

In opposition to democratization, he wanted to see the standing of the bishops strengthened, not by the authority of the apostolic succession, as some theologians who supported him argued, but in order to establish the personal responsibility of the episcopal office, independent of any state authority.

He spoke of the danger that the Ministry of Religion and Education might become a kind of "Archbishop" or even "Pope" if the Church Adviser was appointed. Therefore he pleaded for the strengthening of the Episcopate: "I want no democratically elected church authority to take its place."

In 1932, Berggrav published his views on this matter in an article entitled "The Balance between Church and State." A wide-ranging debate was thereby set in motion between Berggrav and Oftenæs, who was responsible for the Ministry at that time. Oftenæs understood Berggrav's standpoint to be an attempt to give extra power to the bishops, which would not be compatible with a state church. From his side, Berggrav feared that the Ministry of Religion and Education, acting for the state, sought not only decisive influence over the church in matters of administration, but also in matters which were the proper internal affairs of the church. The debate showed that now Berggrav saw the danger of a church constitution vetoed by the state. Some years later, an actual situation arose which Berggrav's foresight had recognized. The strife over the relationship between church and state in 1932 was like a dim shadow forecasting the powerful confrontation during the church struggle a decade later.

The Last Years in Tromsø

Beggrav's last years in Tromsø were among the best of his bishopric. In this period of his life he wrote his most popular book, *Spenningens Land: Visitas-glimt fra Nord-Norge (Land of Tensions: Glimpses of Unknown Norway)*. It became a bestseller soon after it was published (1937) and was translated into many languages in numerous editions. One chapter, "Makkaur," was reprinted in many journals. The book demonstrates how Berggrav related to the natural world and to the people of that area. A good illustration is the story of the chapel of Makkaur. In the autumn of 1934, the Bishop attended a very unusual church dedication. Thanks to their incredible commitment, the 102 people of the village of Makkaur had built a church combined with a school. After the dedication, 13 children were brought to the bishop to be baptized—12% of the population.

Nobody thought that Berggrav would remain Bishop of Hålogaland until his retirement. When in 1937, Johan Lunde retired as Bishop of Oslo; Berggrav still had 17 years ahead of him before his retirement age. Many expected him to become the next Bishop of Oslo.

This time the vote for his appointment was very different from the earlier vote when he was elected Bishop of Hålogaland. No one was surprised this time that he was elected overwhelmingly. For a long time, Berggrav had been recognized as the leader of the Bishops' Conference. Now by this election the popular sentiment was confirmed.

5

The Bishop of Oslo

In 1937, at the age of 53, Eivind Berggrav was appointed to the senior position in the Church of Norway. In his role as Bishop of Oslo he stood at the center of his country's religious and political life.

Berggrav had already shown evidence of leadership in church and state. He was known to favor more authority in the hands of the church hierarchy and less in the hands of the Ministry of Religion and Education. He had already insisted that the bishops—not the Minister of Religion and Education—should determine the suitability of parish priests. The bishops—not the state—should "hold the door" to the church. In this he was following orthodox Lutheran principles, which gave authority to the state in secular matters, but to the church in those spiritual. He accepted that "the powers that be are ordained of God" as Paul had written to the Romans (13:1); he affirmed, in the Lord's words, that the "things that belong to Caesar should be given to Caesar" and the things that "belong to God should be given to God" and not to the state (Matthew 22:21). In these matters he was resolute and defended the right of the church to manage its own spiritual, liturgical, and pastoral affairs.

In 1934, the German churches had been split over this issue when Hitler attempted to "protect" the churches. The Barmen Declaration had insisted upon this independence and made that declaration the foundation of the so-called "Confessing Church," in opposition to the "German Christians" who accepted the control of the church by the Nazi regime. Berggrav followed these events in Germany carefully, and it made him wary of any nationalistic excesses in his own country.

THE CELEBRATIONS OF 1930

While he was still "Bishop of the Arctic," Eivind Berggrav made his views clear about historic nostalgia and national euphoria. In 1930, Norwegians celebrated the 900th anniversary of the introduction of Christianity to their country. A mass gathering of 40,000 assembled on July 29 at Stikelestad where the saintly king Olav had died 900 years before. The crowd was in a fervor of national pride. Some 100,000 more listened with expectation at home on the radio. Berggrav was the preacher and all expected a resounding call for national assertion. Berggrav disappointed them. He did not echo the romantic mood about the past, but warned against such sentimental attachments. He would not look to history to give the national church glamor. The church, he insisted, must deal with the present; its ministry must be the living tasks of today's world. He had no desire to establish the superior office of an Archbishop, as many had proposed. Berggrav's most important work was to fix the place of the church firmly in the present day. This meant taking seriously the challenges of modern thought and modern trends in social life, understanding them, and coming into dialogue with those who considered the church as outdated.

OSLO

For much of its history Norway had not even been an independent country. In 1393, at a meeting in Kalmar, Queen

Margaret of Denmark had succeeded in uniting Norway, Denmark, and Sweden under one crown—that of Denmark. Sweden broke away first and in 1523 the union formally came to an end. Norway remained united with Denmark under a Danish monarch until the end of the Napoleonic wars when the Allies, without consulting Norway, saddled her in an unhappy union with Sweden which lasted until 1905. Before that time Norway's last king had been Haakon VI who died in 1380! With a stab at continuity, five and a half centuries later, Norway chose her own monarch, a Danish prince, and he was called Haakon VII. Eivind Berggrav was 21 before his country became a sovereign independent state under its own king.

Unlike Copenhagen and Stockholm, Oslo had no long tradition as a capital city. Its name was Christiania until 1925. But by the 1930s, Oslo was an up-and-coming capital, affectionately referred to as "the largest village in Europe." There was, however, a long tradition of bishops in the city, of which Berggrav was well aware. His appointment in the Norwegian church at this point in history was therefore a challenge to direct the conscience of a capital city in process of formation, carving out its own traditions. Berggrav wished to do this, not by looking back, but by accepting the present and building for the future.

THE WIDER HORIZON

Although Berggrav was a Norwegian with a great respect for the culture and art of his own country, he was influenced from an early age by the differing cultures and art styles of other countries. As student, journalist, and war correspondent, he knew and appreciated the contributions of Germany, Denmark, and Sweden. He had studied both in Lund and Marburg, with a brief spell in Cambridge. He had read theologians and philosophers from different times and countries. He could look fairly at the disputes between Prussia and Denmark, and during the World War he could sympathize with Germany's point of view. He had no doubt that the Versailles Treaty was unjust, especially in putting the blame for the war entirely upon Germany. Appreciation for men like John R. Mott showed him able to absorb and criticize American evangelical zeal. All this went into the making the Bishop of Oslo potentially a world figure in the universal church.

Yet Sweden was probably the greatest influence in Berggrav's life. Academically, he found the University of Lund (located in the most Danish part of Sweden, Skåne) much more congenial than the University of Oslo. Although a Lutheran, he appreciated the variety of traditions and practices in other denominations and was from the beginning responsive to movements towards unity. It pained him greatly that Christian fought against Christian in the War. He thrilled to the "Call for Unity" issued by the Stockholm Conference in 1925. There he had discovered his mentor in the Ecumenical Movement, Nathan Söderblom. When Berggrav led a Nordic-British Church Conference in 1936 at Vestfold, he was noted as a promising future leader of ecumenical activity.

NATHAN SÖDERBLOM

By 1925, Berggrav had experienced the thrill of an ecumenical conference without having the responsibility of being an official delegate. Like many others, he fell under the spell of the Archbishop of Sweden, with whom he had already cooperated in a Nordic Peace Conference as early as 1917. Söderblom had been appointed to the highest office of the Swedish church in 1914 when he was only 48. The shock of a European war—a *world* war—drove him to work for peace. The young Eivind felt the same shock and joined wholeheartedly in Söderblom's appeal, "For Peace and Christian Fellowship," in November 1914:

> The war is causing untold distress; Christ's body, the church, suffers and mourns. Mankind in its need cries out, "O Lord, how long?"

We, the servants of the church, address to all those who have power or influence in the matter an earnest appeal seriously to keep peace before their eyes, in order that bloodshed soon may cease. Our faith perceives what the eye cannot always see, that the strife of nations must finally serve the dispensation of the Almighty, and that all the faithful in Christ are one. Let us therefore call upon God that he may destroy hate and enmity, and in mercy ordain peace for us. His will be done!

The call was largely ignored; prejudice had hardened and as the bloodshed continued, both sides of the conflict defended the moral rectitude of their position.

The young war correspondent was aware of Söderblom's efforts, and as he witnessed the horror of Christians fighting Christians his interest in peace and the end of *all* war grew. More than a decade later at the "Universal Conference on Life and Work" (Stockholm 1925), Eivind was further convinced that Söderblom was supporting the cause of social responsibility, which he had found lacking in his own church. This explains his undisguised enthusiasm at the time for the "Call to Unity" issued as the conference's message:

The conference has deepened and purified our devotion to the Captain of our Salvation. Responding to his "Follow Me," we have in the presence of the cross accepted the urgent duty of applying his Gospel in all realms of human life—industrial, social, political, and international. Only as we become inwardly one shall we attain real unity of mind and spirit. The nearer we draw to the Crucified, the nearer we come to one another, in however varied colors the Light of the World may be reflected in our faith. Under the cross of Jesus Christ we reach hands to one another. The Good Shepherd had to die in order that he might bring together the scattered children of God. In the Crucified and Risen Lord alone lies the world's hope.

Although it was Eivind's conference message, it reflects the conviction and style of Söderblom. Berggrav's admiration for him grew. In the midst of his trials in the Arctic, he recalled that Nathan Söderblom had learned his lessons in a hard school. He was born not far from the Arctic Circle in the home of a poor country parson, where he observed how ordinary people lived with the trials and sorrows that come to the poor under the stress of a harsh and ungracious climate.

In 1930, Berggrav was active in promoting Söderblom for the Nobel Peace Prize. When the Archbishop died in July 1931, Berggrav went at once to Uppsala to represent Norway at the graveside. His first reaction was, "I find the world has become so poor and heaven so rich." The effect of Söderblom's death on Berggrav was comparable to that of the death of his own father. "It has moved me so powerfully," he wrote, "that from this moment a new chapter begins in my life." In a style distinctly his own, Berggrav compared his experience with that of the disciples on the Mount of Transfiguration. Now, he said, it was for him to translate that experience into the tasks of everyday life.

If Berggrav had not yet been convinced of his future role as a church leader in Norway and on the world scene, he understood that the death of Söderblom had now given him a sign from God. Just as his father's death finalized his decision to become a pastor, the death of Söderblom pointed him towards church leadership, not only as Bishop of Oslo, but also within the Ecumenical Movement. The experience at the coffin of Söderblom was for the young bishop, soon to be called to the high office of Bishop of Oslo, of profound significance. It meant that Söderblom's vision of an ecumenical Christendom and Stockholm's "Call to Unity" never left Berggrav's program. He was destined now to join those few pioneers of the Ecumenical Movement.

In 1963, perhaps the high point of the history of the World Council of Churches, Oliver Tomkins, the Bishop of Bristol, surveyed the Ecumenical Movement in *A Time for Unity*. He listed those pioneers who had made possible the formation of the World Council of Churches (1948) and the expression of its truly worldwide character at the Fourth Assembly in New Delhi (1961). He included Eivind Berggrav as one who guided the movement through its formative years. The list was short; all were American or British names except Berggrav. He inherited the mantle of Nathan Söderblom. All that was to be in the future, but the vision was already clear in 1931. Söderblom had become his second "destiny."

GREEN PASTURES

In the winter of 1933, Berggrav's name was associated with one of the cultural "storm centers" of the period: the American play *Green Pastures*. (The controversy ranged much wider than Norway.) Written by Marc Connelly, the play portrays God as a benevolent, old black man. Some viewed it as an attempt to shock believers, even caricature belief in God. But for many, the play carried them into an experience of real religion. An original feature of the play and one that caused profound theological concern was that God "learned" from experience; his understanding of the world "develops" in the course of the drama. Published and first performed in 1929, the play created a controversy in Norway in 1933. The great majority of church people condemned the play as blasphemous and antichristian; local churches, the university faculty and the liberals all condemned it. But already in 1933 Berggrav was aware of developments in drama that attempted to bridge the gap between Christian witness and secular culture. He saw the play, as many others did later, as an attempt to present the biblical account in a form that would be understood by a generation soaked in secularism.

The play was translated into Norwegian in 1932 and first performed in the National Theatre in Oslo in November. The protest was immediate and a meeting of church leaders and others officially condemned it. It happened that Berggrav was not at that meeting because of a previous engagement in Liselund in Denmark. Shortly afterwards, he went to Stockholm to see the play with his own eyes. He wrote an article for *Aftenposten* about it and concluded that it was not justified to call the play "blasphemous." He saw the value of communicating Christian values in a format that was understood and accepted by those who could not hear the message of the churches. That must have appealed to Berggrav as an example of Christian communication that succeeds. For all its shortcomings, *Green Pastures* was a modern commentary on the biblical truth that "God was in Christ reconciling the world unto Himself."

CULTURAL INVOLVEMENT

Berggrav's involvement as a Christian in the culture of his time was extensive. He was aware of new ideas in literature and even new development in sport! He worked hard at understanding what was going on in the secular society of the thirties. At the same time he was foremost in developing a means to communicate an intelligible apologetic for a Christian faith in a society which was daily becoming more secular. All this involved him in the general cultural debates of his time. He felt it his duty to take part and bring his experience of teaching religion into the discussions of the day. He employed a great deal of his time and energy as bishop to work out new ways of presenting the biblical story and he devised a new catechism.

These efforts aroused controversy. His projects clearly identified him as a church leader who was determined to try new ways to involve the younger generation in the essential teaching of the Christian tradition. Berggrav worked to define a Christian culture even as secularization grew rapidly; the gap between the churches and contemporary culture, he was convinced, could no longer be ignored. The "old" idea of a united Christian society was becoming increasingly lost in the freedom of the individual in a pluralistic society. The tension was evident in new phases of cultural and ethical debates, expressed most forcefully in modern literature through psychoanalysis and sexuality.

It was not only for the sake of the culture that Berggrav

engaged so strongly in the debates, but he also had an apologetic motive. He wanted the church and Christianity to have their part in the cultural life of the nation for two reasons: to fight against the anti-Christian elements in modern art and to enable the church to take up an adequate attitude towards modern culture.

Berggrav also wanted to "correct" the mistakes of the church in its neglect of radio and other mass media. This he did through articles in magazines and newspapers, interviews and radio appearances. From the beginning he saw the value of radio in making known the Christian message. Christian programming, he saw, could influence the people. He very quickly understood how to use radio for this purpose. By broadcasting of church services and talks, through his involvement in discussions and interviews, his voice became known throughout the land. He was often asked to comment upon questions of contemporary art and to give broadcast talks on cultural themes.

In the years between the two wars, Berggrav tried to produce a program of general education as comprehensive as that of Nikolai Grundtvig in nineteenth-century Denmark. At a time when a new worldview was beginning to be taught to the people, disputing the traditional views of the church and of Christianity, he felt it necessary to place the church in the picture and to involve it in the social life of the nation. His purpose was to work for a people's church, broadly involving the whole of life, with a solid Christian foundation. The church must be more than a service institution, providing religious commodities. Unless the church could provide fundamental Christian knowledge and Christian morality on a broad front, the future of a people's church was in grave danger. It is here that we find the central motive for Berggrav's activity between the wars, as bishop and defender of a Christian culture.

SUCH A TIME AS THIS

Scandinavia prided itself upon its neutrality in wartime.

In the madness of war, this part of Europe attempted to keep sane and thus enable the world to seek peace. It was a noble mission. But in 1937, Norway was disturbed at what was happening in Germany—in the church and the nation. Politically, dictatorship was rampant. It looked as though no nation in Europe was able to curb Hitler's reckless ambitions. The Confessing Church, which had been formed in 1934 to preserve the integrity of the Gospel, faced grave dangers. Its best known leader, Martin Niemöller, was arrested and kept in prison for the next eight years. The seminary led by Dietrich Bonhoeffer for clergy of the Confessing Church in Finkenwalde was closed. Those who opposed the national church were discriminated against and sometimes silenced—forbidden to preach or teach in assembly. Youth work in the churches was almost entirely taken over by the Hitler Youth. Resistance to Hitler's idea of a servile church was being broken.

The year 1937 was grave for the Christian Gospel in Germany. Under the leadership of George Bell, the Ecumenical Movement put its weight behind the Confessing Church, but had too little influence either in Germany or on the international scene. The years that followed grew worse. The British and the French soon capitulated to Hitler's plans to take over Austria and Czechoslovakia. In that same year (1938), the fate of the Jews of Europe was made clear on *Kristallnacht* (November 9). Europe drifted to war and Hitler brooked no safe neutrality of any country in his way.

In July 1939, the first martyr of the Confessing Church, Pastor Paul Schneider, was brutally murdered in the Buchenwald Concentration Camp.

"For such a time as this" a church leader was needed in Norway whose vision was broad and who was not afraid to press beyond the boundaries of a traditional churchman. Eivind Berggrav was a man of peace, but he could detect evil when he saw it. For this reason, he worked first for peace and when that failed sought to protect not only the church, but also the culture of Europe with its Christian foundations.

6

Peace Initiatives

The German invasion of Poland on September 1, 1939 and the subsequent declaration by the British Prime Minister that "a state of war" existed between his country and Germany left Berggrav shaken and dispirited. All his hopes to avoid war had come to nothing. He saw only an unmitigated disaster for European civilization and worldwide destruction, morally and economically. But his depression did not last long.

On September 5, 1939, the Bishop of Oslo called together trusted people from his diocese to discuss what the posture and response of the church should be in the present situation. At this point, he thought of a declaration by the church that Christians in Norway should keep in contact with Christians on both sides of the division caused by war and pray for peace. Such a declaration had gone out in 1938 from a group of Norwegian pastors and theologians who were known to be pacifists. Berggrav saw that such a declaration could only carry weight if it had broad backing, and if signed only by the Bishop of Oslo, a declaration would be seen as partisan. He therefore sought out one of the most prominent leaders, with whom he was known to be at opposite ends of the theological spectrum: Ole Hallesby.

Berggrav suggested a strong proclamation, signed by both, calling on the churches to work for peace and the nations to cease from war. At first, Hallesby laughed at this utopian idea. Berggrav knew the difficulties and, after discussion with some friends, redrafted the text and telephoned Hallesby, who now responded more favorably: "Let me hear the text." Berggrav read it and Hallesby replied, "All that seems very good to me. I would like to think the matter over. Give me half an hour and I will ring you back." An hour later Hallesby rang back to say he would sign it. The next day, the Norwegian papers carried the text—a joint proclamation—signed by the two distinguished Christian leaders under the title, "God calls us now." Readers in Norway responded favorably to this unusual statement by such divergent leaders. Berggrav had once again shown his genius in getting the cooperation of people who on most matters disagreed. This was to prove crucial in the later struggles during the occupation of Norway by the Germans.

INTERNATIONAL INVOLVEMENT

Other church leaders, on both sides of the conflict, shared Berggrav's views on war. George Bell, Bishop of Chichester, constantly asserted that the prosecution of war was contrary to the mind of Christ. In 1937, he persuaded the "World Conference on Life and Work," held in Oxford, to include in its message, the following statement:

> The universal church, surveying the nations of the world, in every one of which it is now planted and rooted, must pronounce a condemnation of war unqualified and unrestricted. War can occur only as a consequence and manifestation of sin.... The condemnation of war stands, and also the obligation to seek the way of freeing mankind from its physical, moral and spiritual ravages. If war breaks out, then predominantly the church must be the church, still united as the one Body of Christ, though the nations where it is

planted fight each other, consciously offering the same prayers that God's name may be hallowed, his Kingdom come and his will be done in both, or all, the warring nations. This fellowship of prayer must at all costs remain unbroken. The church must also hold together in one spiritual fellowship those of its members who take different views concerning their duty as Christian citizens in time of war.

Earlier from the German side had come the most spectacular statement of this view by Bonhoeffer at the Universal Christian Council conference in Fanö, Denmark in 1934. Although Berggrav was not there, the statement was circulated and he read and remembered it:

Only the one great Ecumenical Council of the holy church of Christ over all the world can speak out so that the world, though it gnash its teeth, will have to hear, so that the peoples will rejoice that the church of Christ in the name of Christ has taken the weapons from the hands of their sons, forbidden war, proclaimed the peace of Christ against the raging world. Why do we fear the fury of the world powers? Why don't we take the power from them and give it back to Christ? We can still do it today. The Ecumenical Council is in session; it can send out to all believers this radical call to peace. The nations are waiting for it…. The hour is late. The world is choked with weapons, and dreadful is the distrust, which looks out of all men's eyes. The trumpets of war may blow tomorrow. For what are we waiting? Do we want to become involved in this guilt as never before?

Eleven years later, Bonhoeffer was to pay with his life for loyalty to that view. This is not Berggrav's style of language, but he held this view as strongly as Bonhoeffer did.

The emerging World Council of Churches, with much the same attitude to war as Berggrav's, soon discovered his importance. From Council headquarters in Geneva, Nils Ehrenström planned a visit to the Nordic lands and took with him two Germans, Hans Schönfeld and Eugen Gerstenmeier, who would later be involved in the conspiracy to overthrow the Nazis. They soon discovered that Bishop Berggrav was the central figure in the peace initiatives in Norway. As early as September 13, 1939, Berggrav was lecturing in Oslo on "Prepare for Peace." He continued such lectures throughout the country and by the end of the year a collection was published with the title, "The Contribution of the Nordic Lands. Peace now!"

When the deputation from Geneva met Berggrav on October 10, 1939, they invited him to Copenhagen to meet with William Paton, the General Secretary of the International Missionary Council based in London. They eventually met on October 20, talking together with Schönfeld, Ehrenström, and a Danish Bishop, Fuglsang-Damgaard. At this time too an influential group in Norway had worked out a peace plan which it was thought Germany might agree to. The Crown Prince of Norway was involved and the Norwegian Foreign Office. Ribbentrop also knew of the plan, drawn up by the German historian, Ulrich Noack. In it the Czechs were granted independence, separated from Slovakia, and the Polish borders were fixed at the 1914 position. It was thought to be a good basis for negotiating with Germany and acceptable to Britain. William Paton was interested in this plan and suggested that Berggrav might find a way to visit London and discuss this peace initiative with the church and political leaders there.

THE LONDON VISIT

William Paton was a little surprised at the rapidity with which Berggrav took up his suggestions. On December 7, 1939, Berggrav took off by plane from Oslo and, after a brief stop in the Netherlands, was in London the next day! Paton meanwhile prepared a tight schedule of visits.

Among the most important church leaders that Berggrav met were the Archbishop of Canterbury, Cosmo Lang, the Archbishop of York, William Temple, and the Bishop of Chichester, George Bell. He was already well-acquainted with George Bell, who had strongly supported his peace initiatives. The two Archbishops also showed some considerable interest. He was also able to meet other significant persons in political and public life. He was invited to Chatham House, the most influential forum for the discussion of international affairs, to explain his plans. At this headquarters of the Institute for International Affairs, statesmen and academics find it the best place in Britain to explain their views. In its library, Arnold Toynbee wrote his monumental *A Study of History*. Chatham House lectures are famous and "Chatham House Rules" allow a speaker to be frank and even indiscreet, knowing that while his remarks may be used in articles, they will not be attributed to him or her. No political figure of importance, nor any academic, whose field is international affairs, can escape a grueling discussion at Chatham House.

While Berggrav was there, he had the opportunity to talk with Arnold Toynbee. But the real purpose of his visit was to meet the British Foreign Secretary, Lord Halifax. By introduction from the Archbishop of Canterbury, this meeting was arranged on December 15, 1939, at Downing Street. The center of the discussion concerned the Noack document. Berggrav explained that from the point of view of the churches, it was not sufficient to work only with the principles of peace, but that it was necessary also to understand the realities of the situation. Therefore the Norwegian group had tried to get an idea of what would be necessary for the Germans to accept a peaceful solution to their problems.

Halifax asked for an English version of Noack document. Berggrav explained Noack's contacts in Berlin and his position as historian and adviser to the German Foreign Office. According to Berggrav's own account the discussion was calm and practical, though it was clear that Halifax had quite different views from Berggrav on the chances of success.

As usual, Berggrav's mood swung from optimism to resignation. He began to feel out of his depth. The meeting with

Toynbee and the others at Chatham House made him feel quite inadequate. On the day after his visit to Lord Halifax, he wrote to Kathrine, "I am ashamed that I am so often unable to understand what is going on or to see clearly through the ideas which have been put before me in these past few days." He tried to analyze why he had failed.

> I think that I am inclined to make up my mind too quickly. When I find myself on a road I know and feel easy there, I go straight ahead, disregarding all alternative routes. I am not patient enough; therefore I am a poor politician. In my dealings I am too quick. Once I have uncovered something, I tend to assume that that is the only possibility.

Other church leaders did not always welcome these eager initiatives, and opinion on Berggrav was divided at this time. Willem Adolf Visser't Hooft, the General Secretary of the emerging World Council of Churches, was skeptical of his efforts and critical of his "pushy" methods. But William Paton, who knew him far better and was older and wiser than the young Visser't Hooft, wrote a letter to allay his fears:

> I appreciate the fact that Berggrav, being an energetic person, and having a position which gives him some right to speak, wants to make the most of it.... But we must recognize that he is one of the Scandinavian leaders who most fits the place left vacant by Söderblom, and he inspires confidence in people here [London]. In times of such gravity, we have to concentrate on personalities.

A Peace Conference in the Netherlands

Berggrav was fully aware of his impetuous nature and it became evident when he was in London. He saw the value of a peace conference between Norwegian and British church leaders. He had not thought through the significance of such an event, nor consulted widely enough with other leaders, but he had sufficient encouragement to begin arrangements. It was to be in the Netherlands, opening January 6, 1940. Through a contact person in the Netherlands, he obtained the use of a rather fine hotel in Zilven. This was to be *his* conference, but before long the executive committee of the World Council of Churches had more or less taken it over and broadened its scope.

The young and dynamic general secretary, Visser't Hooft, had written to Berggrav on December 9 inviting three leading bishops of Scandinavia to participate as consultants in the Executive Committee. Berggrav was anxious to preserve neutrality, treating both sides in the war equally. He did not want peace at any price. In his memoirs, written in retirement, Visser't Hooft explained the rift between Berggrav and himself. One of the reasons for it is that Berggrav had misinterpreted the views of one of the Dutch delegates who did not mince his words when he described Hitler as basically evil. When Berggrav spoke at the opening session he interpreted this as saying that peace with Hitler meant the end of Europe. Berggrav made it clear that he thought it was possible to change the Nazi regime and he wished to do that. Visser't Hooft noted in the margin of the text of Berggrav's lecture, "All this sounds as though we were still in the 19th century. Doesn't he grasp the fact that there is a demonic element within National Socialism?"

Berggrav met another opponent at the conference, the formidable Chairman of the Executive Committee of the World Alliance, the leader of the French Reformed Church, Marc Boegner. He criticized the Norwegian attitude for its pro-German stance, particularly that Germany should retain her former territory west of the Rhine. In typical fashion Boegner said, "If you give them a bridgehead on the Rhine, it is as though you stamp Germany's foot on our neck while we grovel in the dust. It would arouse a frenzy and you can be sure that at the next opportunity you have bred another war."

Berggrav had the support of the English delegates and those from the Nordic lands, especially Archbishop Eidem of

Sweden. This encouraged him to believe that it was possible to go ahead with his peace plans much as before. Visser't Hooft was less pleased and it was not long before critical voices were heard against the Ecumenical Movement for dragging its feet.

What emerged from this divided attitude of the churches were the different attitudes to the state. Lutherans and Anglicans could understand the German churches far better than those who came from the Reformed churches of France and the Netherlands.

INTERNATIONAL SUPPORT

Berggrav was not the only one seeking peace at this crucial time. He was well aware of the efforts of George Bell in England and he was much encouraged by the proposals of the Queen of the Netherlands and the King of the Belgians to act as mediators in negotiating terms for peace between Britain and Germany. Their proposal was discussed in the House of Lords in Westminster on December 13, 1939. The Earl of Darnley welcomed this and Bell supported him. Bell's speech on that occasion was given much publicity in Scandinavia as well as New York. He opened with a clear statement of his position to anticipate the obvious objections. He had shown his abhorrence of Hitlerism, as he called it, over many years and his work for refugees from Hitler's Germany was well-known. He began with, "I am not a pacifist, nor am I one of those who ask that peace should be made at any price." But he argued that the choice for the nation lay between a fight to the finish which was more heroic, and negotiation, which at this stage might be misunderstood as appeasement. He added, "The heroic alternative meant such a sacrifice, the inevitable extension of the scope of the war, the moral, physical and spiritual exhaustion of the belligerents, perhaps the collapse of European civilization, that no effort should be spared in trying honorably to face the other alternative." Bell went on to endorse the view that this was the time to make peace, rather than wait until "the whole world were enveloped in disaster."

Berggrav took encouragement from this first intervention for peace from England. He was also encouraged by the Pope's Christmas message of 1939 with its "Five Points for Peace." Bell had taken up the Pope's challenge and proposed an ecumenical conference on peace, chaired by the Pope. Berggrav was not out on a limb with his peace initiatives, since some of the best minds in the Christian church throughout the world held similar views.

In England, Bell failed. Yet he persisted in making the point that there was a Germany other than the horrors which Nazism indicated. Berggrav's disagreement with Visser't Hooft had its roots here. Berggrav was increasingly worried by the evil developments as Hitler began to use his power as a dictator, but he always hoped that better elements in Germany could change this. He was right, as Bell was, in detecting that Germany and National Socialism were not identical. Visser't Hooft later learned this too.

German Contacts

Once Berggrav saw that neither the church nor political figures were likely to carry his peace plans much further in Geneva or London, he began to work on a different plan in Germany. Friends in Sweden put him in contact with a German woman of considerable influence. She was Frau Helfferich, the widow of a former Vice Chancellor and Finance Minister in the German Government. Her grandfather was the founder of the powerful Siemens Organization, and the impeccable Chancellor Hindenberg had been a close friend of the family. Frau Helfferich was not a Nazi party member, but she had good contacts at the highest level with party leaders. Together with the politician von Stauss, she arranged for Berggrav to meet with Göring. Von Stauss was also not a party member, but he had a long-standing friendship with Hitler and Göring.

He offered Berggrav the choice of meeting one of these two and he chose Hermann Göring, whom he thought he could more easily influence.

On Sunday January 21, 1940, the two men met. Berggrav was staying in a hotel in Berlin. Göring sent his chauffeur to collect him and bring him to the elegant hunting lodge "Karinhalle" in Schorfheide, not far from Berlin. They talked for two hours. That same afternoon, Berggrav wrote a lively account of their meeting: the Bishop of Oslo and the Fieldmarshal Hermann Göring. The meeting began without the usual courtesies. Göring looked up from his desk and asked abruptly, "What do you want with me?" Berggrav was not offended, but rather amused at the outlandish clothing Göring was wearing. The question was rhetorical. Göring knew full well what Berggrav wanted to discuss and he himself wanted to hear all he could from Berggrav about London's attitude to a peace settlement. He commented on Noack's document. As they talked, Berggrav saw a glimmer of hope. At times Göring sat quietly, at times spoke gruffly. After one period of silence, which Berggrav could not interpret, Göring burst out, "This is an idiotic war!" Berggrav then appealed to his sense of self-importance. He made clear that in England he had found no possibility of peace, while Germany had now the chance to create a new situation and gain the *kudos* from it. He emphasized that something big would come of it. "Germany could line itself up with the whole of humankind," Berggrav noted, "and say to the world: Now, let us all be reasonable. Let us make peace and settle the question of Poland and Czechoslovakia by general agreement." Berggrav went further and said directly to Göring, "You, Herr Fieldmarshal, are the right man for the job. You can seize the initiative and carry it through." This attempt to play Göring off against Hitler misfired. Göring smashed his fist on the table and thundered, "I have sworn my German oath to the Führer and I will abide by it. If the Führer commands I will obey—unconditionally." But after a little thought, Göring described his relationship with the Führer more precisely: "But we discuss with one another every detail. He will say to me, My dear Göring, what is your opinion? I will explain my own view. But I am not prepared to oppose him."

Taken as a whole, Göring's outpouring gave little hope for peace. In spite of that, Berggrav interpreted some details of the conversation as positive enough to discuss them with von Stauss and ask his advice about a return to London for a further conversation with Lord Halifax. In the mean time, he went incognito to Copenhagen, where among other matters he had the opportunity to meet Kathrine who was in Liseland.

FAILURE OF THE PEACE INITIATIVE

Berggrav was once more on his way to London. Many church leaders in close contact with the Foreign Office were not pleased with his visit to Göring. They feared that the German propaganda machine would make capital out of their talks. His attitude at the conference in the Netherlands had also turned many against him, so that he was distrusted. The French, and in particular Marc Boegner, reported to the French Government that Berggrav and his Scandinavian colleagues were "linked to Berlin" and this was passed on to the British Foreign Office by the French Ambassador in London.

After three and a half weeks of uninterrupted traveling for the peace initiative, Berggrav returned to Oslo, disappointed and disillusioned. His efforts for peace were at an end. Yet a slight hope of reviving them appeared in March when an English politician and businessman, Baldwin Raper, asked about Berggrav's contacts in Sweden to help in his own peace initiative. This brought Berggrav into contact with the German Ambassador to Norway, Curt Brauer, and also the Swedish Foreign Minister, Christian Günther. Both encouraged him to go again to Berlin as a last minute attempt. Berggrav took their advice and spent the Easter days in Berlin, largely with Ernst Von Weizsäcker. It got him nowhere and he regarded the visit with a sad pessimism. He described his personal visit to Weizsäcker:

> We met at his home for lunch on Wednesday at about 2 p.m. He was grey and sad. As soon as we were alone, he exclaimed in agony, "There is talk only of war, war, war." He bent forward as though he had just had an accident. The impression was overwhelming.

Weizsäcker probably knew about the planned invasion of Denmark and Norway (Operation *Weserübung*). But Berggrav knew nothing of the danger Norway faced. He had gleaned no such impression from Göring, while Weizsäcker could say nothing. Looking back, Berggrav feared that the Allies would think of him as a betrayer of England to the Germans. Certainly Berggrav's peace efforts were strongly criticized from the side of the Allies. Already in March 1940 the French newspaper *Paris Soir* carried an ironic article with the title, "Grey Eminence in the White Land." It described the Bishop of Oslo and his efforts:

> In truth this Bishop Berggrav is a personality which one rarely meets: a powerfully built fifty-year-old with a good sense of humor, a fresh complexion, lively gestures and eloquent in speech—a man who interests us largely because of the role that he has tried to play on the international scene recently. This Norwegian Primate has perhaps dreamed of becoming an apostle of peace, in that he has tried to establish contacts between England and Germany with the intention of some future peaceful negotiations.

There is no doubt that many rumors circulated about Berggrav's activities, as the following sentence shows: "It is no secret that Herr Berggrav has been on both sides of the conflict, on the one hand with Lord Halifax and on the other with Ribbentrop, Himmler and others who have some influence with Hitler." These rumors would damage him later.

The Mediator for Peace—An Assessment

Berggrav's attempts at mediation failed, and looking back, he could see that they never stood a chance of success. Yet during this period the strength of the man was evident—when he believed in something and had the opportunity to work at it, his powers opened up and his single-mindedness was impressive. For those hectic winter months he must have felt himself in the midst of great international events. His earlier desire to stretch out beyond the boundaries found a new challenge; at the same time, he knew that his participation in the peace initiatives was a last, despairing attempt to avert the catastrophe of a total war. His role was not crystal clear, because he acted both as a private person and also as a church leader. It is doubtful whether he fully realized the dilemma that this double role produced. On the one hand, he had to maintain the strong ethical stance and absolute morality of the church; on the other hand, he involved himself in the political game, maintaining a non-party and neutral attitude for success.

In that time he had to give his heart to reconciliation between peoples of differing views. His political thinking was very much influenced by an ethics of compromise, which often left little room for certain important elements. His judgment of the ideological and political importance of National Socialism remained very unclear, and thus it was easy to categorize the peace mediator as naïve, blue-eyed, and ineffective. But one must not forget that Berggrav represented Norwegian political thinking at the beginning of World War II. He had a task prompted by his ecumenical responsibility as church leader and he did not shrink from it. He must also be seen as the representative of a small nation concerned with maintaining its neutrality. It was neither the first time nor the last that Berggrav would find himself facing a task that put him in a position of difficulty with regard to his church activities, compelling him to go beyond what was normally required of a church leader.

In a letter written to a colleague on October 10, 1939, Berggrav assessed himself:

> The situation can arise when the "powers that be" decide what is the right direction to go, whether it be in the form of a philosophy or a call or in the form of an open expression of an opinion. A child can save a king from a stupid act, but this "child" must become aware that the soldiers of that king can do him harm. I tremble before this responsibility, but one cannot of himself *take away* the power to carry this burden.

He did all that he could to preserve peace and to avoid war. He took the role assigned to him as a Christian leader of a neutral country—to preserve its neutrality and yet to be part of Europe with the responsibilities that carries.

On the night of April 9, 1940, all hope of that peace was ended. Norway lost her neutrality.

7

War Comes to Norway

During the lull in the ground fighting following their victory in Poland, the German military was active on the sea. The German pocket-battleship *Graf Spee* was hunting in the Atlantic for British merchant ships as early as September 26, 1939. It was successful and its commander behaved impeccably—conducting a gentlemen's war and taking great care to protect the crews of the sunken vessels. (The war had not yet reached the bitter stage that all wars reach when human values begin to disintegrate.) But it sunk many British ships and held many British prisoners. Its supply ship, the *Altmark,* enabled the *Graf Spee* to keep at sea by ferrying supplies and fuel; it was disguised to keep it from detection. British Intelligence tracked the *Graf Spee* and in a heroic sea battle forced it into harbor at Montevideo, Uruguay. Three cruisers, although none so heavily equipped with firepower as the battleship, managed to outmaneuver her by their speed. Eventually its commander scuttled the battleship and shot himself.

Prisoners interned in Montevideo told of the presence of the *Altmark,* carrying 299 British prisoners of war. The Royal Navy tracked down the *Altmark* and followed it. It was a difficult task in the vast Atlantic, but it was eventually found in Norwegian territorial waters, north of Trondheim on February

14, 1940. The pursuit, in which the British cruiser *Cossack* violated Norwegian neutrality by entering its territorial waters to attack a German ship that had received permission to follow that course home, was reported like an adventure story. In London British hearts were stirred. Many Norwegians were equally excited by the pursuit. On February 16, the British spotted the *Altmark* from the air. Several ships were involved and a battle between Norwegian and British ships and the German ship ensued. It ended in Jossingfjord where the *Altmark* had been compelled to take refuge. The Norwegian ship *Kjell* tried to stop the *Cossack* entering the fjord, to protect Norwegian neutrality. But the *Cossack* succeeded in boarding the *Altmark* and releasing 299 prisoners, without casualties. Norway protested the action of the British. The Norwegian Minister in London called it "a grave violation of Norwegian neutrality." The Foreign Minister labelled it "the grossest violation of neutrality since the war began" and demanded that "Britain return the prisoners and make due compensation and reparations." The German propaganda experts used the incident to inflame public opinion against the British, accusing them of "piracy, murder, manslaughter [one German sailor had died from exposure to the cold] and gangsterism of the worst kind." The Germans demanded an accounting.

GERMANY'S RESPONSE

The *Altmark* affair explains in part the difference between Berggrav's two visits to Berlin in 1940. When he talked with Göring on January 21, the *Altmark* was sailing home through Norwegian territorial waters. Having deceived the inspectors, it was legally in those waters; guns dismantled, it was returning home after months at sea with no evidence of war prisoners. Berggrav at that time, rightly or wrongly, derived some hope from Göring. By Easter, the atmosphere was quite different with Ernst Von Weizsäcker's comments, "The talk is all of war, war, war." What part the *Altmark* affair played in Operation

Weserübung, the planned invasion of Denmark and Norway is uncertain, but by Easter 1940, plans were well underway.

On April 9, 1940, the Germans practically walked into Denmark—resistance would have been impossible. But they found Norway a tougher nut to crack. Every factor that made Denmark such an easy conquest was lacking in Norway. The mountainous terrain, the difficult internal communications, and the fighting quality of the Norwegian army combined to create a sense of uncertainty in Berlin. The other factor was the strength of the British navy: an invasion fleet, necessary for Norway but not for Denmark, had to face the possibility of a sea battle with a superior British force. However, the German ships landed their troops at the major ports. There was considerable Norwegian resistance, but also uncertainty about the German intention. The Germans had claimed that they were coming to protect Norway from the British. Under certain circumstances and with the recent memory of the *Altmark* affair the explanation seemed plausible. Yet the idea of invading a country to protect its neutrality was puzzling to many.

The confusion is well-illustrated by the landings at Narvik. In the early hours of April 9, the German commander gave orders to his destroyers to enter the Ofotfjord and approach Narvik. The main troop ships were waiting in the relative calm waters off the Lofoten Islands. A Norwegian patrol vessel at the entrance to the fjord flashed the signal that warships were approaching. The Norwegian naval force was hopelessly out-gunned by the approaching German vessels. Their orders, however, were to resist. Then an extraordinary scene was played out. The Norwegians fired a shot across the bows of the German flagship. The German commander sent a launch with two officers to the Norwegians, having first ordered the destroyers to halt. All the finest naval courtesies were observed and the German officer explained that they had come as friends to protect Norway from Great Britain and suggested that he consult his superiors and surrender his vessel. The result was an order to resist. The Norwegian commander called the German officer back and explained that he was ordered to resist. After a courteous departure, the Germans sank the Norwegian vessel with the loss of 180 men. After that, the troops landed at Narvik. The Norwegian army commander decided not to risk the loss of his men.

QUISLING

On April 9, 1940, Berggrav was in Helsinki, Finland. Like most Norwegians, he was completely surprised by the news of the German invasion. The nation reacted at first with shock and anger, then doubts. The Bishop of Olso shared these feelings.

As soon as he awoke to hear the news, Berggrav left Helsinki and returned home via Stockholm. By the morning of April 10 he was in his office in Oslo. Events had moved quickly. On the previous evening, the leader of the tiny Nazi party in Norway had spoken on the radio, welcoming the German visitors and thanking them for their protection. His name was Vidkun Quisling.

The word "Quisling" is notorious today and has entered many languages as a synonym for collaborator. In his biography, Hans Fredrik Dahl offers the following description of the Norwegian politican who led the National Union Party:

> He was a pastor's son, a bright boy at school, although shy and withdrawn. He graduated first in his class at the military academy and later he became a staff officer in the Norwegian Army. His particular specialty was Russian Affairs and he joined Nansen in his work for the victims of famine in the Soviet Union. He was regarded as a humanitarian, with an exceptionally good record among the Armenian refugees, 1925–1927. It was after this that he developed an idiosyncratic form of idealism. It became wrapped up with his growing sense of his own superiority. He was never a Nazi, but his ideas broadly fitted the pattern of "generic fascism." What he saw in the German form of Fascism was a correspondence with his own "Universism," a World Federation dominated by the Nordic race. His attempt

to form a 'nationalist' party in Norway was a complete failure. He never had more than 8,500 members of his *Nasjonal Samling* and failed to gain any seats in the Norwegian parliament *(Storting)*. The German occupation gave him a breakthrough. Quisling's dream was of an independent nationalist Norway united with Nazi Germany to destroy Soviet Communism and lead to, a European Federation, led by the Nordic people. He saw himself as the defender of an independent Norway, but he served harsh occupying powers to the detriment of his country.

Vidkun Quisling announced that he was in process of forming a government. At first, Hitler accepted him, but soon discovered that he was of no significance. He was dropped within days of his meteoric rise to power, but later returned.

BERGGRAV'S ACTION

In such a situation, Berggrav decided to distance himself at once from Quisling, but he was worried about many enthusiastic young men who were ready to take on the German army. Students and others had left Oslo and were preparing for action against the Germans from the mountains in the north. On Quisling, his statement was clear: "Our primary task must be to distance ourselves from everything that Quisling stands for." But those young men in the mountains were in real danger. The Norwegian army was still fighting, but they were protected, if captured, by the Hague Convention. These young men were not. They were without uniform or military recognition. If caught they could be shot.

Berggrav took unwise action to protect them. He went north and appealed to them to give up their struggle and return peacefully, leaving the army to do the fighting. He was personally involved, because his eldest son was among the hotheads! He spoke to them using a megaphone, but it was not just a private action. He had a police escort and the approval of the German Commander, Major General Engelbrecht.

Shortly after seven in the evening, he arrived with his escort in the area. A German standard bearer at some distance from Berggrav asked permission to take a photograph of the Bishop with the megaphone. Berggrav later regretted having given that permission. Witnesses to his message to the young men make it perfectly clear that he was not advising compliance with the Germans, but simply warning against the consequences of their irregular action. The *Police Gazette,* reporting this event, made it quite clear, "We hear that Bishop Berggrav said that the incident had to do only with civilians, who were not in military service. In no way was it a question of calling for a cease-fire in the struggle."

Despite the defense of the action, there is no doubt that it was unwise and impetuous. Making such a journey in the context of the German invasion and with the support of the German General Engelbrecht was bound to be interpreted as complying with, perhaps collaborating with, the will of the Germans. Berggrav made this doubly suspicious when he followed it up with a radio broadcast next day, appealing to civilians not to involve themselves in the armed struggle. Again, he appealed to the Hague Convention, quoting those sections dealing with irregular armed groups of civilians, urging Norwegians to be law-abiding, and not to carry arms, nor to use violence in the form of sabotage. "Let us show discipline," he said. It did not help matters when he added that he had met among the Germans many who were good and courteous.

German propaganda made good use of the incident. The German newspaper *Signal* carried a copy of the photograph showing Berggrav amidst the snows of the north with the caption, "The Norwegian Bishop of Oslo, speaking to the front line of the Norwegian soldiers, through a megaphone, declares the uselessness of fighting against the all-powerful German armies." On April 17 the German newspaper *Völkischer Beobachter* published a statement that the Bishop was ready to work with them. This, together with the picture in *Signal* damaged Berggrav's reputation among patriotic Norwegians.

As this German newspaper was on sale in the kiosks of Oslo in May, Berggrav felt an apology was called for. He went to see the Minister of Information and insisted that no such notice should be allowed to appear again. He was assured that his wishes would be respected, but as he later said, "my satisfaction with the interview was perhaps a little premature."

In other parts of the world, too, Berggrav was thought to be a collaborator. Both at home and abroad, the impression was given that Berggrav was not to be trusted when he denied the reports about him at the end of April. The photograph which first appeared in *Signal* was reproduced in many Allied publications.

BERGGRAV'S STRATEGY

From his point of view, Berggrav saw the need to move carefully and, to a certain extent, cooperate with the German occupying power. He would not, however, cooperate with Quisling. Yet faithful to Lutheran and Pauline theology, he recognized that "the powers that be are ordained of God," instituted by God to preserve order. Under his leadership, the Norwegian church, during the first few months, carried out a policy of cautious collaboration, on the basis of international law for occupied nations (Geneva Convention). During this period, Berggrav and his colleagues took the opportunity to consolidate and plan the strategy of a "unified church."

Solidarity was not going to be easy in the Norwegian church. Strong historical and theological divisions existed within it. Yet aided by the common revulsion at the German treatment of Norwegian democracy, Berggrav was able to fashion a united church front. As in his earlier peace appeal, he was able to cooperate with pietistic leaders, who previously had looked upon him with skepticism. Together with other church leaders from the small Catholic and Free Church groups, they formed a new, unofficial council for consultation. This *Kristen Samraad* planned the resistance and led the Church Struggle on two fronts: first and foremost, to fight for social justice and human rights, but also to fight for the freedom of the church in a totalitarian state.

Berggrav did not allow the church to be on the defensive, waiting until it was attacked and then compelled to defend itself. He wanted the church primarily to defend justice and liberty of conscience and to condemn both injustice and violence. The church did this, often quite effectively. Its action for human rights attracted the attention even of those who had had little to do with the church. Many Norwegians now saw the church as the best voice for justice, truth, and freedom.

In these ways, Berggrav challenged the Nazi regime head on. Later, when conflict with the state arose, the church was intact and ready.

THE KING AND HIS GOVERNMENT

The German policy for their occupation of Norway was like that in Denmark—to establish the monarch as a puppet sovereign. The king was, in fact, presented with an ultimatum, which had serious consequences. The courageous and disastrous story of April 1940 resulted in many difficulties for Berggrav.

On April 10, the day after the invasion started, the German Minister in Oslo, Curt Brauer, visited King Haakon in his rural base at Elverum. On the previous day an effort had been made to capture the King by the German air attaché, with a company of paratroopers. The commander had been so confident that he boasted, "With this company I could get the devil out of hell." He failed and the king remained safely in Elverum. Brauer presented the King with an ultimatum: surrender and we will protect you and your dynasty; refuse and we shall bring the full force of Germany's military might against Norway. The king pointed out that this was a grave issue which he could not decide himself. He asked to consult his ministers. Brauer left, but before he reached Oslo he had his answer. The King consulted his ministers. They were divided, but followed his lead. He put his reply to Brauer in writing:

> I am deeply affected by the responsibility laid upon me if the German demand is rejected. The responsibility for the calamities that will befall people and country is indeed so grave that I dread to take it. It rests with the government to decide, but my position is clear. For my part, I cannot accept the German demands. I have carefully examined my mind and my position and find that I cannot appoint Quisling Prime Minister, a man in whom I know neither our people as a whole nor its representatives—the Storting—have any confidence at all. If, therefore, the government should decide to accept the German demands, and I fully understand the reason in favor of it, considering the impending danger of war in which so many young Norwegians will have to give their lives—if so, abdication will be the only course open to me.

It was a message of defiance to the Germans and rejection of their demands. The government followed the courageous lead given by their King. The people of Norway heard of the government's decision by radio from a local station. Before long, the battle for Norway involved British and French as well as Polish troops. Yet the German military prevailed; to the great disappointment of the Norwegians, the allied troops withdrew on the night of June 3, 1940, leaving Norway to face the Germans for the next five years. The Norwegian commander, General Ruge remarked bitterly, "So Norway must go the way of Czechoslovakia and Poland," adding, "But why? Why withdraw when your troops are still unbeaten?"

The battle for Norway was eventually lost. But resistance continued while Hitler was triumphant in the rest of Europe. After Paris fell and the British retreated from Dunkirk, there was no further help from allied troops. Even the Royal Navy was stretched. There would be greater massacres as the war went on, but casualties in the Battle for Norway were not inconsiderable. The heaviest casualties were among the

British—between 4000 and 5000 men and several warships. But at sea the Germans suffered the greater defeat. Hitler was delighted with the brilliant success of his armed forces, describing the battle for Norway as "not only bold, but one of the sauciest undertakings in the history of modern warfare." What he did not say was that at the end of the fighting, Germany had only one heavy cruiser and two light cruisers fit for action. Churchill said of this that it was "of major importance, potentially affecting the whole future of the war." The resistance continued and Churchill set up a special agency to give what support he could to the freedom fighters.

NORWAY HAS A MASTER

While battles flared along the extended coast of Norway, another battle was developing behind the German lines—a battle for the hearts and minds of Norwegian people.

After Quisling's brief period of glory, the Germans appointed a *Reichskommissar* for Norway, who virtually had complete authority over all civilian matters. He was a typical choice, the forty-one-year-old Joseph Terboven, a functionary who owed complete loyalty to the Nazi Party which he joined in the 1920s. He rose in the ranks until in 1933, when Hitler came to power, he was appointed Gauleiter of Essen. The Führer trusted him and promoted him from Gauleiter to *Reichskommissar* of Norway.

Terboven arrived in Oslo on April 24, 1940. His first proclamation was unambiguous: "By order of the Führer, I have as *Reichskommissar* taken over for the duration of the Occupation." Norway's master had arrived. He had two initial tasks, first to advance Germany's war effort and second, to organize a government inside Norway that would be pliable to German pressure and capable of controlling the Norwegian population.

He began with a direct censorship of the press and radio, control of the telegraphic system and soon persuaded the government he formed to call for King Haakon's abdication. This call did not have the support of the Norwegian people and the King knew that. He refused to abdicate, but remained in London, closely in touch with affairs in Norway, largely through Stockholm. Berggrav was not surprised when an attempt was made to silence the pulpit and to put an end to circular letters, which were encouraging Norwegians to oppose the Nazi government. One such letter read, "Thou shalt obey King Haakon … thou shalt detest Hitler … thou shalt regard as a traitor every Norwegian who keeps company with Germans or Quislings at home … thou shalt despise treason and remember that its punishment is death." The letter continued to list "ten commandments." Such letters helped to sustain the Norwegian population during the summer of 1940.

Berggrav was clearly behind the efforts to distance the church from the Nazi government of Norway and he acted most effectively when the pulpit was attacked. In April 1941, the government *(Riksraad)* addressed instructions to the Norwegian churches.

> In the present situation, it is required, pending further notification, for all pastors, whether they are party members [the Nazi Party] or not, to emphasize in their proclamation that which is purely edifying and eternal in the Gospel, so as to present the church's worship services from being affected by political divisions, which are a tragic reality among our people.

The pastors as a whole could not accept such interference with their preaching. The seven bishops of Norway put their signature to a letter drafted by Berggrav. The letter insisted that the church must not withdraw to a state of inwardness and piety, nor can it, even under the present circumstances, allow the Word of God to be interpreted by social, national, or particular political interests. The clergy and other servants of the church would not accept ideological and political guidelines telling how the Word of God ought to be proclaimed in given situations. "The eternal Word," they affirmed, "should shed light upon what is foremost in our daily life and in the lives of all of us."

It was clear to Berggrav that the church department of the Nazi government was afraid of the open pulpit in which the concrete application of the Law of God and the teaching of the Bible might undermine Nazi authority. Like the Confessing Church in Germany, the Norwegians later set up a "temporary church government," which, when up to 130 pastors were arrested, could put laymen and theological students into vacant pulpits to assure that the Word of God would be proclaimed and its demands and promises made clear.

THE RETURN OF QUISLING

The summer and autumn of 1940 had seen Germany in control of most of Europe. Constant pressure was now applied to Norway to declare itself a republic and invalidate the authority of the Royal House. In September, Terboven persuaded his docile parliament to adopt these measures. By the end of that month he had established by fiat a new commissariat government staffed and entirely controlled by Quisling supporters. Terboven did not trust Quisling, nor did he name him among the new Ministers, but Quisling was leader of the Norwegian Nazi Party. Terboven, still doubtful about Quisling, declared a one-party state and that party was Quisling's. From the end of September onwards, the Norwegians had no elected representative in Oslo. All was set for totalitarian rule.

Terboven's first attack was on the law. In November, the new Minister of Justice declared that his office alone had the right to appoint or dismiss jury members and other court officials. After this he decreed that any judge, including those presiding over the nation's highest courts, could be forced into early retirement if the Minister of Justice believed that it was for the good of the country. Only Terboven retained authority in legal matters, acting through the subservient Minister of

Justice. Faced with Terboven's ultimatum, all members of the Supreme Court resigned. Berggrav took note.

THE NORWEGIAN CHURCH STRUGGLE

The German word *Kirchenkampf* (church struggle) was known throughout the world church, associated with such names as Karl Barth and Martin Niemöller. Berggrav was well acquainted with it, but recognized that any such struggle in Norway would be quite different. The obvious difference was that Norway was a country occupied by the Germans and it was patriotic to resist. Yet there were other marked differences. In Germany the church was divided between the *German Christians* who were subservient to Hitler and the *Confessing Church* which defended the purity of the Gospel and the freedom of the church. Both of these church entities were threatened by Nazi indoctrination. The German *Kirchenkampf* was essentially a theological one, although it carried social and even political overtones. In Norway, thanks to Berggrav's astute policy, the greater part of the Church of Norway was united in the resistance, from the first a defense of human rights, freedom of conscience, and the liberty of the citizen. It was, of course, also a theological resistance, done in defense of the freedom of the church.

The church struggle in Norway can be said to have started in January 1941 with a letter from Berggrav, addressed to the Minister of Religion and Education, appointed for Nazi sympathies. The letter expressed dissatisfaction with the injustice and violence in the behavior of the puppet government, as well as making a strong objection to the pressure which the government was bringing upon the clergy in order to break their vow of confidentiality.

This letter, drafted by Berggrav in consultation with his fellow bishops, was signed by all the Norwegian bishops. It went even further raising the question of the legitimacy of the state on the basis of the Augsburg Confession:

As the Confession indicates, the church stands in a definite relationship to the *just* state. This presupposes that the State, through its constituent bodies, maintains law and justice, both of which are God-given orders.

The bishops were pointing out that according to the Augsburg Confession, a state must be a legitimate state, i.e., a just state, before Christians can be expected to be obedient and loyal. They have no obligation to obey an unjust state.

During 1941 there were a series of controversies between the Bishops, and the Ministry of Religion and Education. The policy of the Ministry was apparent:

by concentrating preaching upon purely spiritual matters, the church was to become detached from the affairs of the world;

religious instruction in the church schools was to be impregnated with Nazi doctrine;

to split the College of Bishops and to place Nazi sympathizers in the most important church offices;

to discredit pastors who were opposed to the occupying powers and replace them with "loyal" pastors.

The Ministry tried to take over a number of episcopal functions and to strengthen its authority within the church. Theologically, the leading personality among the staff of the Ministry, Dean Sigmund Feyling, was strongly influenced by Paul Althaus, who in Germany had argued for a positive attitude towards the Nazi state by the church particularly in his book *Church and State according to Luther's Teaching*. The Ministry represented a view of the totalitarian state, which was incompatible with the common law and human rights.

On February 1, 1942, by the "State Act of Akershus" (Oslo), Vidkun Quisling assumed power over the church as Minister President, declaring himself to be the Supreme Bishop of the church. As such, he denounced Bishop Berggrav. He also replaced the Dean of Trondheim with a loyal supporter of the

Nazi Party. The Bishops protested, as they also did over a new law that enrolled young people in a Nazi youth organization in order to indoctrinate them. All this was a repetition of what was going on in Germany, where the majority of Lutherans accepted and only a minority objected to these new laws. In Norway, the balance was different.

Before the month was out, the seven bishops resigned from their offices *as church administrators*. They thus broke administrative contact with the Ministry of Religion and Education. But they continued to operate as bishops in the care of the clergy of their diocese. A kind of "free church" was thus created, with majority support. Among the clergy, 93% followed their bishops and resigned their administrative functions.

As the German Confessing Church had done with their Barmen Declaration in 1934, so the Norwegian clergy read their confessional document aloud from their pulpits on Easter Day, April 5, 1942, and declared their resignation from administrative office to the people.

The Easter action was planned by Bishop Berggrav and his unofficial Christian Council. It clearly separated the office of ordained ministry from that of church administration. He denied that they had become a free church, although it looked like it. This is what Bonhoeffer wished to do in Germany, but he received no support, not even from Karl Barth. The Norwegians argued that the resignation of the clergy was a temporary break with an unjust Nazi state, not a separation from the state church constitution.

As far as possible, the bishops and clergy continued to fulfil their pastoral responsibilities, but without accepting any salary from the state. They renounced every official status. Wedding ceremonies, for example, were no longer held in churches. This strange "free church" or "people's church" had to create its own peculiar temporary organization in order to address the ecclesiastical and political emergency. For a period of three years the Church of Norway functioned separately from the state administration of religion. It was not easy and the Nazis caused as many problems as they could. But the church, liberated from the state administration, had the support of the people.

A CONFESSION AND A DECLARATION

When a Lutheran Church takes up a position of disobedience to the state, it has to have good reasons and the rationale must be theologically sound. The statement made to the churches in Norway on Easter Day 1942 was backed by a carefully discussed and drafted document. Its principal editor and influence was Bishop Berggrav, but it was drafted during the week before Easter Day after wide consultation with theologians and others of the church. Luther's doctrine of the two kingdoms required strong theological arguments to justify the church's resistance, based upon Paul's teaching of the obligation to obedience by Christians before the secular authority.

During the resistance in Norway, Berggrav read several of these attacks upon Luther and knew that they were being widely used. It angered him and he gave several lectures in 1941 showing how differently Luther had spoken and written. The word "servility" does not apply to him! The lecture, which he gave in many illegal church meetings, was titled, "When the coachman goes mad: Luther on disobedience to civil authority."

Writing in the Foreword to *Luther Speaks,* a collection of essays by Lutheran pastors published after the war, Berggrav gave several examples of the way in which Luther had guided the bishops and clergy in their resistance.

> I remember a time when we were in doubt in our circle as to whether we should use the word *tyranny* in connection with the Nazis in one of our appeals. Some thought that this was unnecessarily defiant and provoking. All we had to do then was to turn to Luther and use a quotation from him: they couldn't very well put Luther in prison!

Luther called to the tyrannical rulers:

The sword is at your throats if you so much as think that you sit so fast in the saddle that no one can throw you. Such certainty and such obdurate presumption will be the cause of you breaking your necks—one day you will experience this!

Berggrav looked back to the guidance given by the New Testament and by Luther as he and the clergy asserted their right to liberty in a totalitarian state.

The document that became the "Confession" of the Lutheran Church in occupied Norway, like the Barmen Declaration in Germany (1934), was written in the style of the classical Confessions of the Lutheran Church. It was a solemn, authoritative document, that defined the church's faith and ministry in a difficult situation. The Germans of the Confessing Church deemed such a situation to exist in 1934 with the rise of the German Christians. The Norwegians under Berggrav felt the need for a similar type of confession when the Nazi state exceeded the limits of its power over the church and exercised a tyranny over the people. It was called *Kirkens Grunn (The Foundation of the Church),* and its subtitle was *A Confession and a Declaration.* A careful study of that document shows how solid a foundation was laid for a Lutheran resistance to the unjust secular state.

THE FOUNDATION OF THE CHURCH

The principal theme of this confession was the independence of the church from the state which required the Lutheran doctrine of the two kingdoms to be reinterpreted by the church leadership. The confession is directed against the church policy of the Nazi state and is marked by a polemical tone. It is also an attack upon the nazification of the people and the ideology of National Socialism as a whole.

The key section, however, is Article V, "The correct relationship of Christians and of the Church to the Secular Authority." Here it is emphasized that both church and state, the spiritual and the secular authorities, have their calling from

God. They have no right to interfere in the proper functioning one of another. "Both of them—each in its own way—should serve God among the people." The document clearly stated, "Therefore, we confess that it is a sin against the Lord God when either of them seeks to impose a regime in which either claims to be the lord of the other."

This separation of the two kingdoms does not mean that the service of the church to the state and the people is ignored. The Norwegian church leadership saw the responsibility of the church to include judgment upon the righteousness of state actions and advice to the people on their obedience to the state. From a theoretical point of view, this doctrine does not mean that the two kingdoms are identified with the church and the state, but in practice this is the way it functions.

A strong point in the interpretation of the doctrine of the two kingdoms in *Kirkens Grunn* and other documents of the church struggle is that God is the Lord of *both* kingdoms. It is a gross misinterpretation of Luther to assign to the two kingdoms two different lords. Such dualism is in total contrast to basic Lutheran teaching. With one quotation from Luther, the Norwegian bishops limited the functions of the secular power: "The secular power has laws which stretch no further than over life and property and that which pertains to 'earthly' life. For God will not allow any other power but his to rule the soul. There are also many other powers but his alone rules the soul."

This confessional declaration made it perfectly clear that there was a right to refuse to obey a totalitarian state. Quoting Luther again, the document stated, "When the secular power attempts to interfere in the spiritual realm and wishes to take the conscience captive, where God alone sits in judgement, then one should not obey them." By way of commentary, *Kirkens Grunn* further notes, "The church must take its stand upon Scripture and the Confessions in every case where totalitarian demands are made upon the conscience and where one is compelled to disobey the law, but always on the basis of the Word of God and the Christian conscience."

LEGITIMATE REVOLT

Berggrav's action against the state was legitimized by his theology. He began with a clear distinction between a just and an unjust society, not as a matter of personal assessment, but based upon a theological definition of the just society, a constituent part of which was the natural law. This gave him a clear definition of *the just state:*

> The just state acts in accordance with law and justice, which is anchored in God;
>
> The just state is limited to temporal matters, and is not allowed to influence matters of faith and conscience;
>
> The just state has to promote law and justice in the society and keep brutal and crude power under control;
>
> The just state is able to distinguish between the good and the evil deed, and causes no difficulties for the good deed.

Berggrav adhered closely to Paul's teaching in Romans 13 and interpreted it to mean that law stands between the citizen and the state. If the state respects the sovereignty of God's law, then every citizen is obliged to obey the state as though he were obeying God. But without God's law, there can be no proper authority. All this is good Lutheran teaching, but he goes further and says that where there is no law and order the Christian has a fundamental right to revolt.

Dietrich Bonhoeffer had already faced this dilemma. Was he going beyond Luther in saying this? Bonhoeffer was convinced that Luther's teaching led to this conclusion. His summary was identical with that of Berggrav and there is no evidence that they influenced each other. Where there is a breakdown of law and justice, the Christian has three tasks: to warn the unjust state of the judgment of God, to aid the victims, and ultimately to revolt if there is no other way to change. Whether both Lutherans fell back on "Reformed" models is open to question. They were both very convinced Lutherans.

Both made a contribution to political ethics by a theological assessment that the people have the duty to judge the legitimacy of the state. That is democracy, theologically based.

THE PERSECUTION OF JEWS

Like the Barmen Declaration in Germany, the Confessional Declaration of Norway was silent about the persecution of Jews. Both had a paragraph about the treatment of the Jews and the anti-Semitic propaganda in an earlier draft, and both cut it for tactical reasons. In Germany, where Bonhoeffer had helped to draft that paragraph, the omission of the paragraph led him away from the Confessing Church and to conflict with it. Berggrav was also concerned. Like Bonhoeffer he had made earlier protests. In the summer of 1941, he protested against the condemnation of mixed marriages with Jews and on the basis of Galatians 3:28 protested against this racism, maintaining that all races are of equal worth. The Bishop made it quite clear that any attempt by a people or a race to assert its superiority to other races is contrary to the constitution of the church. A few months later, the Dean of Trondheim made a strong protest against the plan to confiscate Jewish property.

In the middle of October 1942, the Nazis began to take steps against the 1800 Jews in Norway. A few weeks later, on November 10, a letter of protest was read out in all the churches of Norway, signed by the entire church leadership. It was the only public declaration by the churches collectively against the persecution of the Jews throughout the entire period of the occupation. The letter stated that the Jews were being punished for their biological origins, a denial of their human rights, and contradiction of the plain Word of God: "Were we silent on this legalized injustice against the Jews, we should share responsibility and guilt for this injustice." They appealed to Minister President Quisling, in the name of Jesus Christ, "Stop this persecution of the Jews and bring to an end the racial hatred which through the press is spreading in our land." Although Helmut Von Moltke had warned the Norwegian resistance movement as early as September 1942 that action was to be taken against the Jews, about 42% of the Norwegian Jews lost their lives, mostly in German concentration camps. Many of those who lived were rescued by dramatic escapes to Sweden. The resistance movement, including the church, acted too late to prevent the massacre.

The church's protest, however, was not without effect, helping many inside and outside its walls to see more clearly what was happening; it encouraged a general resistance among the people against the horrors of the Nazi regime. More than anything else, the persecution of the Norwegian Jews opened the eyes of the Norwegian people to the true nature of Nazism.

BERGGRAV AND THE EASTER DEFIANCE BY THE CLERGY

While the Confession *Kirkens Grunn* was being drafted, the authorities began to pay close attention to Berggrav; the Bishop of Olso was aware that the net was tightening around him. Rather than spending most of his time in the episcopal residence, he began to stay in his holiday cabin, which the family had bought in the 1930s, situated in Asker, well away from Oslo. In the house in Oslo there was a cellar room, where Kathrine's personal possessions were stored during her stay in the hospital. Berggrav brought the papers connected with the various drafts of *Kirkens Grunn* for safety into this private room to prevent them falling into the hands of the Nazis. And yet he felt more than once that they were not safe from the Nazis even there. Consequently on Palm Sunday he burnt several papers including earlier drafts of *Kirkens Grunn*.

He knew that it was only a matter of time before he would be arrested. That very morning, Palm Sunday, 1942, he received news that his sermon, "Our Salvation," was to be stopped, and although the Good Friday service might continue, he was forbidden to preach. That evening, when he went in to Oslo he received a letter from the State Police, signed by R. W. Kranz. The letter contained not only the order forbidding him to preach but also not to leave his house during the Easter period. This meant far more than no preaching during the days of Holy Week, but that he could not even attend worship like any ordinary churchgoer, as he confirmed when he sought out Kranz in his office. The purpose of this was to isolate Berggrav, whom they had rightly assessed to be the leader of the whole church resistance. Although the authorities had forbidden him to go out from his dwelling, they did not succeed in cutting off his links with his followers. Berggrav tried every means of secret meetings. Yet as he saw the State Police posted outside his cabin at Asker, he knew that his movements were curtailed and that the success of the church struggle would now depend upon others. Good Friday, therefore, marked not only a turning point in Berggrav's life, but also in the progress of the Norwegian church struggle.

When the *Kirkens Grunn* was read out from hundreds of pulpits in Norway on Easter Day, the one who more than anyone else had been responsible for drafting the script sat in his cabin in Asker, unaware of how the proclamation was received.

8

House Arrest

When Eivind Berggrav was arrested on April 8, 1942, several other members of his "Christian Council" were also taken by the police to prison. They were incarcerated together, but Berggrav, as the chief offender, was placed in a solitary confinement cell. He was no stranger to prisons, because of his earlier work as prison chaplain. But now he realized the loneliness of the solitary prisoner. In his notebook he wrote:

> The footsteps of one after another went by, doors were opened and shut from cells opposite: I heard one stop and knew that someone was standing there and could look at me through the spy-hole, as one looks at an animal in a cage. Yes, freedom became for me a crying need.

Two days later, he was brought before the Minister of Justice. He was accused of making false declarations about the police and circulating seditious letters to the other bishops. Berggrav did not find the interrogation very frightening. In his diary, he wrote of it as "amusing" and "rather disappointing." Had he known what was going on behind the scenes he might have been a little more disturbed. In the newspaper *Fritt Folk*, Quisling denounced him as the political ringleader of an insurrection and, of those Berggrav led, he added, "These people must be treated without scruple and punished for what they are, cheats and traitors. Because of their behavior they must be hanged, disposed of."

This was no empty threat. A few hours before he was interrogated, Berggrav's death warrant was ready to be signed. Few could have predicted that the hard line of Quisling, which nearly succeeded, would be changed so rapidly. Berggrav's strategy of playing the Norwegian Nazis off against the Germans bore fruit. His contact person appears to have been Theodore Stelzer, a friend of Count Helmut Von Moltke, who in his official capacity could approach the authorities in Berlin. When Moltke and Bonhoeffer went on their mission to Denmark and Norway, their intent was, under the guise of official business, to rescue Berggrav. When they came to Oslo on April 13, they were not able to visit Berggrav in prison, but they sent him an encouraging greeting. Writing in his *Memoirs*, Berggrav said—somewhat sarcastically—that the "freedom" he had won when he was released from prison lasted about one and a half minutes. He left the prison as a free man at 4:30 p.m. on the afternoon of April 16, but immediately, three policemen took charge of him and his son Oivind and drove them to their home. Berggrav was told nothing. But Quisling had won a partial victory. The world believed that Berggrav was freed. But for three years he was under house arrest in his cabin in Asker.

LIFE IN THE CABIN

Berggrav had no idea that he would be in his cabin for three years. At first, he joked about his stay in the "prison" that he once looked upon as a holiday retreat. From his veranda he could see three men outside the cabin, including the local police chief of Asker. He quipped, "Here there are more guards than prisoners." Soon the seriousness of the situation dawned upon him. About nine in the evening, a column of uniformed men arrived and unpacked their rucksacks to settle down for the night. By now there were ten guards and among them a young enthusiast from the Norwegian Nazi Party, who was in command of the guards. It was clear that the purpose was to isolate Berggrav. Every contact between him and the outside world was to be cut off, including with his family. The intention was to set the principal representative of the church struggle outside the conflict.

For some months, a military-style watch was manned by a random selection of local police who were not well-disciplined. The authorities were worried about the ease with which Berggrav might get through the circle of guards designed to isolate him. For this reason, the instructions for guarding Berggrav were precise and strict. There were 13 paragraphs under the heading "Instructions for the Police Guard of the Granstua" (Granstua was the name of his holiday cabin.). The commander of the guard employed twelve men, three of whom would always be on duty around the cabin. The cabin would be locked and only the commander would have possession of a key. The guard must be close. Paragraph 7 said categorically that "All visits are forbidden." To this rule there was to be no exception. His wife, who constantly sought permission, was allowed to visit only once.

Paragraph 6 insisted that "guards must under no circumstances enter into conversation with Dr. Berggrav. All requests must be referred at once to the commander." This should have meant that for three long years Berggrav had conversation with no living soul except the commander of the guards, but soon his son was able to come to spend time with him. Berggrav was also greatly comforted when the housekeeper came; soon he engaged her in conversations. When Berggrav's wife was released from hospital, she asked if she might share his imprisonment with him. Her request was never answered.

Paragraph 10 had the following instructions: "Dr. Berggrav may be permitted to go outside for a specific time, but only within an area carefully marked with red upon the map. The guard must have him constantly under surveillance and there must always be two guards on duty." That meant that

Berggrav was confined to the immediate vicinity of the cabin and that police or soldiers were never more than a few meters away from him! Other paragraphs were equally strict. Berggrav had no doubts about the limits of his freedom. But because the guard was generally made up of Norwegian police, he could maintain a good relationship with the men, saying often, "You are only doing your duty," "No hard feelings," or other encouraging words.

Berggrav became a sensation in captivity. It was reported in the Swedish press that a whole company of guards had been converted by him, so that they had constantly to be changed. This was, of course, strongly exaggerated. Yet there was a grain of truth in these reports. Berggrav gradually built up an extraordinarily good relationship with these "guards," so that they dealt with him ever more freely and his contacts with the outside world were greatly improved. Not all of them were party members. He came to designate some of them as "good wardens" and they took considerable risks to help him.

BREAKING THROUGH THE IRON RING

Berggrav did not accept his confinement "without a fight" and he soon found ways of getting out of the cabin. He made himself a key, so that he could go out while the guards were sitting on the sunny side of the house. His first adventure was about the end of July when the need for freedom overcame him. He had a longing to see the sunrise from a hill nearby. The sun rising over Oslo on a clear morning was a sight he loved to see from the top of Vardaasen. In July, he planned to see it again. One evening, he squeezed out through the kitchen window when the guard was busy on the opposite side of the house. He quietly laid out his sleeping bag, with other essentials, in the woods not far from the house. He could see from the stars that it would be a clear night and morning. Then he climbed the hill and from the top of Vardaasen saw the sun rise over Oslo. He stayed there, enjoying his coffee, and returned about 6:00 a.m. He had an anxious half hour in the woods outside the house waiting until the way was clear, so that he could get into the house without being seen. It was a wonderful experience, he noted later, and an unnecessary risk, but typical of his actions.

Later he was even bolder, particularly after he had acquired a police uniform with the help of one of the "good wardens." He took great care to hide and secure the uniform. At first, he thought of it as a protection. When the war ended, he thought, the prisoners would be shot and he among them. Dressed as a policeman, he could escape. But later, he saw the value of the uniform as a disguise when he wanted to travel into Oslo.

During his three-year period of house arrest, he made at least four visits to Oslo, dressed in one or another disguise. Each visit was for a specific purpose. Once it was for a meeting in his own Oslo residence, a meeting in the secret *Kamin*. For that visit he wore a false beard and glasses. At other times, he arranged meetings in his own cabin. Alex Johnson tells of one of his meetings with Berggrav:

> I received precise instructions on a typewritten note: "train at such and such a time to Asker, main road to Drammen, first path to the left." At a precise point on the way, I should turn off to the right and walk forty metres. I counted my steps, stopped, and looked around. Berggrav came out laughing from behind a bush, dressed in an old pair of trousers and an equally old jacket. "Follow me!" he said, and he smuggled me into the cabin. I was left with some documents at the table while he made coffee. Then suddenly the door opened and a fully uniformed policeman stood there demanding to know where the Bishop was. He threatened, "You know where he has gone. Tell us at once or we will make you talk. We have our means to make you talk." Then he added, "What are you doing here?"
>
> I spoke rapidly, confused and frightened. Then the policeman pulled off his beard and glasses; it was

Berggrav. I have not laughed so much for a long time. But Berggrav became serious and pointed out the dangers.

Alex Johnson remembers it as a wonderful evening.

Berggrav carefully concealed a radio in his cabin. With it, he could keep himself informed about the events of the world outside. His first concern, however, was with what was happening in Norway itself. He knew from experience in Germany how Nazi power was established. Its progress was predictable, following as far as possible the pattern so successful in Germany. First, legitimate government—Hitler was democratically elected and supported by the universally-honored Hindenberg. Then Hitler addressed the church, which he "protected" and tamed. After the church he turned his attention to the schools and youth movements; the young must be won for National Socialism. They must believe their destiny lies with the State, with the *Volk*. To his massive youth audiences, Hitler would say, "You are nothing; the *Volk* is everything." Finally, Hitler demanded the extermination of the Jews and all who were not purely of the Aryan race. The weaklings and inadequate would follow.

Berggrav had seen all this happen in Germany before the war. Norway was next. Berggrav himself was in confinement because he had prevented Quisling from "protecting" the church. The battle now raged over the schools.

THE BATTLE FOR THE MIND OF THE YOUNG

After his aborted six-day rule at the beginning of the invasion, Quisling was reinstated with great ceremony at Akershus Castle on February 1, 1942. He assumed the office of Minister President. One of his first acts was to establish a "Teachers' Front" on February 5. Membership was obligatory for all teachers. In his official organ, *Fritt Folk*, Quisling announced that the Teachers' Front "will serve as a straight jacket for all those who are unwilling to do their duty for the State and for Norwegian

Youth." Teachers were also strongly advised to become party members of the *Nasjonal Samling* (the Norwegian Nazi Party). At the same time, he issued another decree establishing a Nazi Youth Movement, modeled on the German *Hitlerjugend*. He defined his purpose: "give us control of 400,000 young people from whom we shall select those who are to be trained for membership in our party."

It was clear that Quisling saw this as only a beginning of a process, which would eventually give him control over other professional bodies. Berggrav saw this—with alarm—as an exact pattern of the Nazi methods he had observed in Germany. It took some time for the underground movement to decide what to do. Eventually, a letter of rejection was drafted and sent on February 20, 1942. This same organization that had been formed in the previous year to bypass the German censor wrote to every teacher in the country. The result was incredible: 12,000 out of Norway's 14,000 teachers rejected the Teachers' Front.

Quisling acted quickly. Within a week, arrests began. Orvar Saether, formerly the chief of the hated *Hird* strong-arm force, who had been appointed *Führer* of the Teachers' Front, took personal charge of the arrests: 200 in Oslo, 200 in Bergen, 100 in Trondheim, and hundreds more in smaller towns throughout the country. By the end of March, Quisling had more than 1300 in custody. Most were held in the Grini concentration camp, just outside Oslo. Quisling now used the threat of forced labor, side by side with Russian prisoners of war in the Arctic, to break their will. Almost 700 teachers were selected for transportation. They were packed in cattle wagons, as Jews were in Germany, and sent to the concentration camp at Jorstadmoen. Conditions there were terrible—constant labor, inadequate food, physical harassment, and isolation from friends and families. Under such pressure, only 50 out of 687 teachers had a change of heart. The miserable tale of ill treatment continued, but the great majority of teachers did not falter. All this time, the schools were closed and Quisling had to give way or face a collapse of education in the land. The teachers were a tougher tribe than he had reckoned.

But this did not happen until after Berggrav's imprisonment. He had followed the attempts to break the teachers with deep concern, both because of his own interest in the education of the young and the close relationship between church and education.

Those teachers who had not changed their mind, more than 500, were then put on an unsafe ship designed to accommodate 250 under appalling conditions. Despite protests even from Nazi sympathizers, Terboven gave the order for the ship to sail from Trondheim to Kirkenes on April 14. There they were treated as criminals.

Berggrav was not too preoccupied with his own condition to follow the plight of the teachers. He began to see that it was possible to win against the Quisling government. By the beginning of May, the schools were reopened and many of the teachers returned to their teaching without mention of the Teachers' Front. In the autumn of 1942 the forced laborers of Kirkenes were freed and allowed to return to their teaching duties. But then Quisling turned to the Jews.

THE PERSECUTION OF THE JEWS IN NORWAY

When the Germans invaded, less than 1500 Jews lived in Norway; about 350 of whom were German Jews, refugees from Hitler's anti-Semitic regime. The Norwegian Nazis were not especially anti-Semitic until the Germans came. Quisling then began to follow the practice of his masters. By June 1941, when Germany invaded Russia, all Jews in northern Norway were arrested and sent to forced labor in Arctic camps. In February 1942, the letter "J" was stamped on all identity papers held by Jews, and in the summer of 1942, four Jews in Trondheim were executed without trial for "spreading news" about the war on the basis of BBC broadcasts. Listening to the BBC was a crime for all Norwegians, but the death penalty seemed to be reserved for Jews. By September 1942, Norwegian police began to arrest Jews on flimsy charges, but most Jews felt that conditions might improve and, apart from a few hundred who fled over the border to Sweden, the majority went on with their everyday life as normal. Then an event occurred which gave an excuse for the full Nazi treatment. In October, a Norwegian policeman was shot by the leader of a group of Jews escaping to Sweden. The Nazi papers made much of it and demanded "an end to the Jewish problem in Norway." There followed a series of arrests, confiscation of property, and a reoccurrence of the infamous *Kristallnacht* in Germany.

Although under house arrest, Berggrav was sufficiently in touch with the church resistance to see to it that the clergy lodged strong protests. A group of bishops and professors sent a personal petition to Quisling begging him to intervene on behalf of the arrested Jews. A circular letter was sent to all clergy trying to arouse public opinion against the treatment of the Jews, denouncing anti-Semitism as unethical and contrary to the tenets of Christianity. This pastoral letter had the marks of Berggrav upon it. Berggrav's deep concern about the persecution of the Jews was fully expressed in the action of those Christian leaders who could protest openly, just as had been his concern about the teachers.

It is not difficult to imagine how he accomplished his participation in the development of this pastoral letter and the personal letter to Quisling. He had been very careful to plan the safety of his visitors, disguising his own absence and having the help of neighboring families near the cabin. He even managed to celebrate his 60th birthday in one of the neighboring homes.

Securing the Relative Safety of his Cabin

Although there were long periods of loneliness, Berggrav was able to have visitors and occasionally to travel, usually in disguise. The travel was the most dangerous. Disguises are usually easy to penetrate, but the room where he slept was also vulnerable to being found empty or to being invaded when he had visitors. To avoid such interference, he employed a strategy which was successful.

One dark night at the beginning of his incarceration, he forced open one of the windows and hurled a log with all his might into the surrounding woodland. It naturally caused a stir among the guards, who thought the Bishop had escaped. They searched, but could find no trace of him. Then one of the guards came up the steps into the house, only to encounter Berggrav in his nightshirt at the top of the stairs, indignant at being disturbed. "Is it not enough," he protested, "that I am kept here under house arrest, against the law of the land, that it should now be necessary to disturb my night's sleep? Is there no limit to your persecution? Aren't twelve men with their commander able to keep an old man in check?!" The guard was most apologetic and gave his solemn word that he would not disturb him again in the night. From then on, Berggrav could consider himself relatively safe in his own house.

Berggrav had a certain impishness about him. Despite the obvious dangers, he enjoyed dressing up and fooling the guards or frightening his friends. In fact, when it was all over, he kept the disguises and on at least one occasion, he fooled his son. On New Year's Eve after the war was over, the whole family had assembled in Blommenholm where his son lived. Berggrav arrived with his false beard, pretending to be a Swedish engineer. For quite a time even his own son did not recognize him.

It would, however, be quite wrong to think of Berggrav's three years as a series of lucky breakouts and adventures. Mostly he was alone and for long periods of time he could not get out. Everything depended upon the goodwill of the guards and especially of the commander. Not all were understanding in the same way and, even when Berggrav had the sympathy of the guards, there always existed the potential unannounced visits of their superiors. These visits sometimes coincided with the presence of friends in the cabin. He was lucky to be able to smuggle them undetected into hidden corners of the building. But these were often close calls which generated a nervous anxiety in Berggrav, one that told upon him.

As people need people, Berggrav suffered greatly from the long periods when he had no one with whom to converse. For a man of controversy as he had always been, conversation and even argument was his lifeblood. Any person who has been in prison for a length of time knows the terrible loss of such contact with friends. Berggrav felt it more strongly than most. He wrote extensively, but this was not enough. He even smuggled letters in and out, but he longed to sit down with his friends to smoke and talk, worrying out together the issues of the day without anxiety. Many issues in the church needed such relaxed conversation. He pondered over the Teachers' Front and even wrote about it. He felt the pain of the Jewish persecution and needed to meet with his fellow bishops to plot action. Sometimes this was possible, but its absence deepened his loneliness.

Berggrav attempted to overcome this loneliness by leading a disciplined life. He proceeded like clockwork and divided his day into precise units—so much for sleep, so much for physical exercise, so much for writing, etc. He became an extraordinary good cook. "I never missed a meal or a shave," he said, "in order to retain my self-respect."

His daily schedule was as follows: 7:30 a.m. rise, breakfast and reading; 10–11 a.m. work outside, such as chopping wood; then working on his writing until 12:30; lunch at 12:30 p.m., then an hour's rest in bed; and relaxation until dinner at 5 p.m. After dinner, he would work at his desk again, with coffee, and go to bed at 10 p.m. The day ended with his reading in bed until he fell asleep. By keeping strictly to this timetable, Berggrav was able to keep boredom at bay.

THE BEGINNING OF FAMILY CONTACTS

Officially, Berggrav had very few opportunities to contact his wife. She could not visit him and in the first few months of his incarceration the only contact was a weekly letter to Kathrine, which was carefully read by the police and censored if necessary. She was permitted to reply and this exchange of letters is a valuable record of Berggrav's time in house arrest; but they were not allowed to discuss "actual issues" in these letters. On one occasion, Kathrine managed to get through the police prohibition by writing simply that the text for the Sunday preaching was from Luke 4, the Sermon at Nazareth, which contains the statement, "He has sent me to preach release to the prisoners." Berggrav warned her not to quote the Bible again, quipping "it is much too relevant."

After a few months came a private regulation about visits which enabled him to meet his wife, other members of the family, and some neighbors in the houses surrounding the cabin. Despite this, it was a lonely existence when one considers the unusually active life he had been living. In the "Song of the Lonely Man," which later became well-known even outside Norway, he described his anxiety and deprivation, the silence and the loneliness, but also the joy which greetings and presents from his friends gave to him. It ends with a confident tone, "God, how near you come to me when I am completely alone."

THE WRITING PROGRAMME

Berggrav had been a fluent writer all his life but he had never had so much quietness or unoccupied time to give to his writing until he was imprisoned. During these three years his talent had full play. He wrote hundreds of pages and smuggled some of the more political pages out of the cabin. Other writings were quite harmless and were used to cover up the more controversial themes. Among these harmless writings were six biographies of churchmen, which were published in one volume in 1946 under the title, *Norske kirkeprofiler fra siste sleksledd (Profiles of Norwegian Churchmen from the Last Generation).* He also worked on a translation of part of the New Testament into Norwegian, which had long been his concern. Shortly after becoming chairman of the Executive Committee of the Norwegian Bible Society in 1937 (he had been a member of the Board since 1927), he raised the issue of a new Norwegian translation, a project that was initiated in 1939. He had a particular interest in the Letter to the Philippians. The war held up the work of the Bible Society, but Berggrav used his time to draft some parts of his translation. After the war, the work was taken up again by the translation committee and Berggrav saw it through when he continued as chairman. He did not see it completed, but by 1978 it was published and is in use still.

Other writings during these years needed to be hidden and kept secret, including an account of his journeys for peace before Norway was invaded, the origins of the war, and the development of the church struggle. Of considerable importance were his detailed suggestions for a post-war constitution for church and state. As early as 1946, his *Kirkens Ordning i Norge (A Church Constitution for Norway)* and *Staten og mennesket (The State and the Individual)* were published.

Much discussion ensued in Norway about the future of the Norwegian church and its relation to the state, as well as the role of the state in relation to the rights of the individual. Berggrav could not fully take part in this, but he had ways of communicating his ideas and comments on documents smuggled to him. During the autumn of 1943 and until the spring of 1944, many illegal letters passed between Berggrav and the lawyers, theologians, and bishops who concerned themselves with this future planning. It was by no means a harmless theme and many risks were taken. Letters sometimes got into the wrong hands. Berggrav attempted to include the views of many international figures in these discussions—Friedrich Meinecke, George Jellinek, and even Harold Laski. Berggrav was in good standing with the lawyers and his son Otto was able to bring to him current literature on these themes.

One of Berggrav's strengths was his ability to see themes in historical perspective. He was not content with seeing the future in relation to the end of the Nazi occupation. He needed a broader historical sweep: "We can understand our present far better when we look again at our past," he wrote. His words are sharp and pointed, and his description of the demonic elements in the amoral society are brusque and uncompromising. Berggrav declared that the state had betrayed the inherited ethical and religious values of the country, leaving the foundations of the moral order in ruins. These inherited values had their roots in the divine reality of human life. He maintained the theological basis of natural law. At the same time he also warned against the misuse of religion by those such as Hitler and Quisling. With clear references to the party programme of *Nasjonal Samling* (Quisling's party), he exposed the misuse for propaganda purposes of basic Christian words and values: "The new Machiavellianism of the 1940s claims to be the upholder of truth, every time they lie; to uphold human rights when they subjugate; to demonstrate love and compassion, when they torture." These manuscripts obviously had to be hidden from the Nazis.

In the early summer of 1943, something happened which made him even more careful. His son, Dag, informed him that a letter from Arne Fjellbu to the Bishop had been confiscated by the state police. For a week or so Berggrav expected a house search and hurriedly collected all the incriminating papers and burnt them. When the police eventually searched his cabin, they found only harmless theological or devotional documents.

Not all his writings on state and church were lost in this preventative holocaust. Sensitive material already had been copied and smuggled out. Berggrav's intention was to publish it when the war was over. A proof copy in Sweden of *Staten og mennesket (The State and the Individual)* was translated into

English, German, and Swedish. A key figure in this operation was Harry Johanesson of the Sigtuna Ecumenical Institute, where at Pentecost, 1942, the German conspiracy was revealed to George Bell, the Bishop of Chichester.

THE GERMAN CONSPIRACY: THE MEETING WITH VON MOLTKE

Years before the war, a powerful group in Germany, representing the army, the church, and the political world, were working for the overthrow of the Nazi regime. What appeared to be their most successful moment in 1938, when Hitler met with Neville Chamberlain in Munich, failed because of Hitler's unexpected success in gaining control of the Sudetenland in Czechoslovakia. After that disappointment, the conspirators persisted, although weakened once war broke out. The entry of America into the war in December 1941 gave them renewed hope. Two centers of this conspiracy were the *Abwehr* or military intelligence and the *Kreisau Group,* meeting at the estate of Count Helmut Von Moltke. It was at a meeting on Pentecost, 1942, that George Bell met with Dietrich Bonhoeffer at the Sigtuna Ecumenical Institute. Hans Schönfeld from Geneva was also there and expressed similar sentiments to Bell. The full plan was to overthrow the Nazi regime and replace it with a temporary military government. Could Bell persuade the British to deal honorably with a non-Nazi government in Germany and negotiate a peace treaty? Despite Bell's efforts, the British refused, although for a time, Churchill was interested. In 1942, Berggrav knew nothing of this, but he was to learn about it in the following year in a remarkable meeting with Count Helmut Von Moltke.

On the night of March 18, 1943, Berggrav met in his brother's house in Oslo with Von Moltke, Colonel Steltzer, and Arvid Brodersen, who was much involved in making Berggrav's writings known. At that secret meeting, Berggrav learned of the efforts of the German conspirators to affect British opinion and inform them of "another Germany," one being as opposed to the ideology of Nazism as the British were themselves. He learned that this was Bell's mission also. In many speeches in the House of Lords, and in many newspaper articles, especially *The Times*, Bell had argued with convincing zeal against the Nazi regime and for the "other Germany." As Von Moltke outlined his views, Berggrav agreed with the purpose, but did not believe it was possible to persuade the Allies to take a different view of Germany.

Berggrav's diary notes that they also discussed the question of the future of Europe after the war, a discussion in which they were more agreed. Among the members of the resistance movement in Germany was strong support for the creation of a federal Europe. This idea appealed to Berggrav and influenced his writings at the time, especially *Staten og mennesket,* where he dealt not only with the rights of the individual in a national state (Norway), but with international human rights and their role in a Federal Europe. It is interesting to note that when George Bell came to Sweden in 1942, it was not to meet Bonhoeffer, about whose planned visit he knew nothing. At Sigtuna, he was taken completely by surprise. He was sent by the British government to find out all he could about the attitude of the Scandinavian churches. His diary shows that his questions were persistently about conditions in Norway, Denmark, and, even more, the situation in Finland. It is thought that Churchill had a proposal for a North European Union, including the Scandinavian countries and Britain. However, the Soviet Union was clearly still a problem in these discussions. Bell's sympathy for Finland showed that he regarded them as more of an ally than an enemy. Of the Soviet Union, Bell thought much like Churchill: "With the Soviet Union we have nothing in common but our enemy." In Berggrav's discussions even Von Moltke thought that the time was not ripe for including the Soviet Union in a European Federation. "That must wait for at least 200 years," he said. In his diary, Berggrav comes again and again to this question and in two places (August 5, 1943 and July 27, 1944) he clearly expresses his concern that the Soviet Union could threaten the independence of Norway after the war.

Some of the issues discussed during that long night with Von Moltke were far too dangerous to enter into his diary. After the war, however, he was able to disclose them. By then Von Moltke had been executed.

They had discussed the assassination plots against Hitler, which Bonhoeffer had supported. Von Moltke, on the other hand, was totally opposed to assassination, even of Hitler! At a lecture on Luther in 1941, Berggrav had dealt with the theme of tyrannicide and concluded that under certain specific circumstances it could be justified. But despite this, he saw a strong objection to the actual event:

> One must, first of all, be quite clear that there are not other ways by which the same purpose could be achieved. Assassination can only be in the last resort. More important than getting rid of Hitler is to find a new leadership which opens the way to freedom. My objection at that time was that it was now too late to dispose of Hitler.

A fear was present that assassination might create a new Hitler legend; on this Berggrav and Von Moltke agreed.

For Berggrav, after a year of house arrest, this conversation with a leader of the German resistance was a breath of fresh air. It gave him new inspiration. "That was the shortest night I experienced throughout the whole period of the war," he wrote. It was with greatest sorrow that he learned of the massacre of the whole resistance group after the July 20, 1944, assassination attempt which miscarried, allowing Hitler to survive. Although Von Moltke was totally against the assassination plot, he was executed also, but not before he had forced the accusing judge to admit that he was condemned for being a Christian. After this historic meeting and long before he knew of the execution, Berggrav expressed great admiration for the personality of Von Moltke. Yet he was fearful of the dangerous situation in which the German resistance movement found itself.

THE PRICE OF FREEDOM

From many sides efforts were made to persuade Berggrav to give up his hard line in the church struggle. The first attempt came on Friday, August 14, 1942, when a verger—an attendant to ecclesiastical or political officials—from western Norway suddenly appeared at his cabin with a proposal for a peaceful and reconciling solution to the church struggle. The verger told of discussions he had with leading personalities on both sides of the struggle and presented his plan for reconciliation. Berggrav was naturally very skeptical. He wanted nothing more than to be free, but without conditions; so he hesitated, asking for time to study the proposal more closely.

This first initiative contained no changes from the attitude he had encountered during Holy Week. Again, a further attempt to persuade him offered nothing. The chief of the State Police came in uniform and personally offered him immediate release on condition that he signed a document saying he promised not to do anything, either publicly or privately, in his religious functions against the leadership of the *Nasjonal Samling* or the Germans. These conditions were quite unacceptable to Berggrav and in his written reply he said that such conditions would be in contradiction to his ordination vows.

A year later the police chief tried again and this time with an offer to travel to Germany with his wife. Neither of them wanted this and Kathrine obtained a medical certificate to say that she was not well enough to travel. At the same time, Eivind and Kathrine Berggrav were put under severe psychological pressure. Kathrine was even threatened. On the night of Whit-Monday, three men sought her out, threatened her, and accused her of being involved in political activity; her telephone service to the house was cut off. The whole episode was frightening for her.

The resistance movement in Norway *(Hjemmefront)* wanted to help Berggrav escape to Sweden or England. As early as Christmas 1942, plans were drawn up to overcome the guards and rescue Berggrav. In November 1943, an envoy from *Hjemmefront* visited him, but was not able to persuade him. Nonetheless, towards the end of February 1944, preparations were being made for his escape, and after a meeting with his wife in the woods, he decided to remain under house arrest. In a letter to his son Otto written the next day, he explained why he had turned this offer down: "It would have been a stolen joy," he wrote, "if we were to fly to another land." This was inconsistent with his approval of the flight of the King, but he could see the critical difference. King Haakon kept the government intact. He was not in exile, but merely ruling Norway from London. Berggrav could find no parallel activity for himself in exile. He saw the need to remain in Norway during the occupation if he were to take his leading part in reforming the Church of Norway after the war.

It was such reasoning that persuaded Dietrich Bonhoeffer to return from the safety of America in order to be with his people during the war and be accepted in the church after the war, when fundamental reforms would be needed. Berggrav was fortunate that he survived; Bonhoeffer did not. Berggrav smuggled a letter out to his king explaining why he had to stay and combat the forces in Norway that would harm the church. A few months later, he received a greeting from King Haakon in which the king expressed the hope that the Bishop would have the courage "to hold fast in a struggle which the whole world watches with admiration and the hope that they would meet again in a free Norway." Berggrav took this to mean that he must stay put.

Berggrav had become a symbol for Norwegian freedom and independence, not only in Norway, but throughout the free world. The Christmas issue of *Time* magazine displayed his picture on the front cover and inside was a long report on the story of Berggrav and Quisling. An even grander proposal to feature Berggrav in a Hollywood film was hinted, but he would hardly approve of that!

The talk of a rescue went on particularly as the end of the war seemed in sight because a real danger existed that the Germans might kill Berggrav in a final period before surrender.

In the summer of 1944, Berggrav's son Jan fled to Sweden and then on to England to avoid compulsory service under the Nazis. A few months later, Berggrav had a further offer to effect his escape. He remained and then had the hardest Christmas of his life. On the morning of December 20, 1944, his 19-year-old son Dag was arrested. On the same day, one of the guards who had become a close friend was shot. This was the lowest moment of his life. He recorded that the worst thing about that Christmas was that he could not pray. It was not that he did not believe in God anymore, but something far worse: "Every time I tried to pray, I was confronted with hellish mockery: 'You know, all right, that it's no use; they'll torture the young man in spite of your prayers.' " Alone in his cabin, by the sole light of a flickering candle, after the storm had passed, he experienced the most difficult Christmas Eve of his life, scarred by temptation and doubt. Facing profound temptation, he fell back upon Luther, from whom he had learned to pray aloud even defiantly! He took his New Testament, read the Christmas story from the Gospels aloud and experienced, despite everything, a sense of peace entering into his soul. This experience confirmed what he had often preached, that the Christian life is not built upon feeling, but upon faith and confidence in the Word of God. And yet, he was still deeply worried and the opening weeks of the New Year, 1945, were the worst. It helped a little that Pastor Dagfinn Hauge could assure him that his son was safe and a German pastor had telephoned Kathrine to say that one of the German Gestapo chiefs had assured her that the young Berggrav came to no harm. All plans for an escape had already been abandoned for fear of reprisals against the son. Later in 1945, Berggrav was reasonably sure that the Germans would not hand Dag over to the Norwegian Nazis.

Once again he put his trust in the difference between the *Nasjonal Samling* and the Germans.

THE ESCAPE

Around Easter 1945, the question of an escape was raised again and this time it was in earnest. On April 12 the final preparations were made. London had given the green light to the resistance movement that they bring Berggrav out safely. On April 16, Berggrav left his cabin with his son Otto about 8:30 in the evening and took the train to Oslo, getting off at an unmanned halt, before the main Oslo station, where he was to meet the Swedish Consul. In Oslo there was a house belonging to a close friend of the family. The first part of the plan was carried out without difficulty, but within a few hours the escape was discovered and all the members of the family had to take cover. An attack was timed for half an hour past midnight. Then a group of young men from the resistance stormed out of the woods and overpowered the guards. Later in the morning, a telegram was sent to all police stations that a group of armed men had overpowered the guards and that Eivind Berggrav was freed from imprisonment. The plan was a complete success. But the leadership of the *Hjemmefront* feared that Berggrav had been killed by Quisling's thugs, while the police thought he had already escaped to Sweden. By April 24 rumors circulated that he had been seen in Stockholm, others that he had spoken on the radio from London. To add to the confusion, the left wing of the resistance movement circulated the information that Berggrav had been set free and that he was now safely in the hands of the Communists! The Bishop was not at all pleased to hear of these rumors and he feared the action of the Nazis.

But he had greater fears than that about his son, Dag, who was still in the prison at Akershus. The danger was that he would be handed over to the Norwegian Nazis, as the war was going against Germany, or that they might release his son in order that Dag would lead them to him. Berggrav made every effort, including a bribe of 30,000 kroner, to discover the truth about torture and abuse. It was a time of great distress.

But three weeks later came the liberation, the end of the war, and the family was united at last. Even the youngest son, Dag, was released from Akershus.

Kathrine had suffered greatly during this period. Berggrav spoke of it after her death: "For mother, it was the greatest burden of her life." The liberation was not the joyful celebration for which the family had hoped. The following weeks and months brought yet more tears of bitterness. Much had changed over the past three years, and in the following year Berggrav had to examine every aspect of his experience, even the way in which he was himself regarded by the people of Norway.

Even after the liberation, bitter moments of recrimination still existed. Norway had changed and many were critical of Berggrav. His action with the megaphone was not forgotten, while most of his activities during his captivity were simply unknown. His attempts to bring peace in the months before the invasion were looked upon with suspicion. But within the church his position was secure; he was recognized as the Primate of Norway. In the Ecumenical Movement he was a symbol of resistance and endurance. He was widely recognized well beyond the boundaries of his own land.

In the years of endurance he had faced hard trials which had helped him achieve a better understanding of himself. But there is no doubt that he was physically weaker. Above all, the experience had concentrated his mind on and strengthened his belief in the freedom of the church and the sovereignty of justice. As the war came to an end, he was ready with a programme for the rebuilding of church and state in Norway. However, the post-war years turned out to be very different from what he and many others had thought it would be.

The Rape of Finnmark

Berggrav retained an affection for the northern provinces of Norway all his life. The suffering that Finnmark endured as the fires of war smoldered out gave him deep anxiety and pain. The Russian troops overwhelmed Finland and compelled the weary Finnish army to turn their guns against their former allies the Germans. Finland declared war on Germany early in October 1944. As the Germans could not predict what the Red Army would do after clearing its own northern territory of German troops, steps were taken to preserve its 20th Mountain Army in Norway. Anticipating the need to withdraw from Finnmark, a scorched earth policy was decided upon. As he retreated and by the direct command of Hitler, General Rendulic, the German commander in North Finland, ordered every building, house, and hut in Finnmark to be destroyed, all stores of food and equipment, and all livestock to be moved or destroyed. The entire population was deported en masse. "Anyone who stays behind," he added, "will perish in the Arctic winter." Terboven issued his own decree:

> The evacuation necessitates the removal of the civilian population, as the enemy has proved that in those territories occupied by him he ruthlessly and brutally forces the civilian population to give him active assistance in achieving his aims. This means that no other means of existence of any kind must be left to the Bolshevic enemy in the fighting zone. All installations, such as housing accommodation, transport facilities and food, must be destroyed or removed. The population in these districts will be deprived of the bases for their existence, so that in order to be able to survive they must evacuate to those Norwegian territories, which are still protected by the German Wehrmacht. He who does not comply with these unequivocal instructions exposes himself and his family to possible death in the Arctic winter without house or food.

The German 20th Mountain Army was in full retreat by November 1, 1944, but remained intact in southern Norway.

As they retreated, the orders were carried out ruthlessly. Norway's own chief of police hurried to support the Germans, warning all civilians that, if they fell into Russian hands, "it would mean murder, plunder, terror, rape, atheism, and moral degradation." The destruction of Finnmark then began in earnest. Special Army demolition squads, assisted by units of the Norwegian Nazi *Hird* organization, trailed behind the main troop units, destroying everything in their wake. Town after town fell victims to Hitler's scorched earth policy. Hammerfest was first. Destruction began on November 3; within two days, it was a dead city. Soon all Finnmark was ablaze. The inhabitants were either forced on to boats to travel southwards along the coast or struggled along the National Highway 50 behind the retreating German army. By the end of the year, 43,000 Norwegians had been evacuated.

Into this pitiful state, some members of the Norwegian Government came back to Finnmark and began to assert sovereignty over the land. The German 20th Mountain Army made good its withdrawal. Units were still in fighting shape with their equipment intact and their men under tight control, ready to make a last stand. Then Germany capitulated and within a short time, Red Army troops withdrew from all Norwegian territory, much to the surprise of many Norwegians.

On May 8, Joseph Terboven followed Hitler's example and committed suicide. With the capitulation of the Germans, the Norwegian Nazi leader, Vidkun Quisling, surrendered himself freely to the police. The resistance movement came out into the open. Norway was free and the post-war period began.

9

The Liberation

Even at the end of 1944, German strength in Norway was impressive. Hitler insisted that only the best trained and well-equipped units should defend "Fortress Norway" against the British invasion which he was convinced would come. Consequently, German troop strength in Norway never fell below 300,000, and by Christmas 1944, it rose to more than 400,000 when the crack 20th Mountain Army began to arrive from Finland. While it seemed obvious on mainland Europe, and even in Denmark, that the German military force had been broken, in Norway this was by no means clear.

Berggrav was still under house arrest as 1945 dawned. On January 1 he began to write a New Year's message, later published in *Kirke og Kultur,* on an assessment of the coming year, in which he expected liberation for Norway. He confronted his readers with a balanced estimate of the possibilities for the church in the post-war years. He used an optimistic tone, tempered with a warning of dangers to come. He presented three fictitious characters: the plausible pessimist, the cautious optimist, and the "man of the church," who would depend upon human relationships and most of all upon that profoundest of relationships, "the human search for God."

He saw that all exuberant talk of a new spring in the church would need to be modified and false predictions exposed. He predicted (and so it proved) that shortly after the end of the war church attendance would decline. The bond between people and church, which had held firm for those five difficult years, would weaken. But he was cautiously optimistic.

THE DAY OF HOPE

In the early days of May 1945, the Germans were laying down their arms, but in Norway an uncertainty lingered. On May 5, General Boehme, the German Commander-in-Chief in Norway, had under his command an undefeated army, entrenched in easily-defended positions. The war may have been burning itself out in the rest of Europe, but General Boehme was determined to maintain an active defense and make a last stand in Fortress Norway. After the German capitulation, Boehme could not be reached during May 6th and 7th. It is difficult not to be moved by his emotional address to his troops over Radio Oslo, once he received orders telling them that all military operations were to cease:

> This capitulation hits us very hard, because we are unbeaten and in full possession of our strength in Norway, and no enemy has dared to attack us. In spite of all that, in the interest of all that is German, we also shall have to obey the dictates of our enemy. Clench your teeth and keep discipline and order, obey your superiors. Remain what you have been up to now: decent German soldiers who love their people and homeland more than anything else in the world.

The resistance fighters came out into the open and met no opposition. The Germans proved more than willing to cooperate in a peaceful transition of power.

The bells rang out in the churches and the national flag of Norway replaced the German swastika. Norway was free and independent. Berggrav described the day many times, but most vividly when he was addressing a meeting of Bible Societies in 1946, faced with the enormous task of producing Bibles for Europe and bomb-shattered Germany. He portrayed that day as beginning in bitter despair and most everyone expecting a civil war. It ended, he said, with a white plane flying overhead to say that peace was coming. He added, "It was like a revelation of how God can change a situation on this earth." His cautious optimism was obvious when, looking at the devastation in Europe and the immensity of the task of renewal, he said, "We who had the experience of those days in the spring of 1945 should be the last ones to be frightened of an emergency like this."

At that time many visions of how Norway would rise again were afoot. All political parties had plans for renewal and engaged in a wonderful spirit of cooperation. A group of leading personalities from many aspects of the country's life together drafted a letter to the government *(The Future of our Culture),* expressing the hope that solidarity in support of spiritual values and the basic elements of the national culture would flourish.

THE BISHOP OF OSLO

It was expected that Berggrav would resume his position as Bishop of Oslo and Primate of Norway. But many people noted that he was much changed. The incarceration had left its mark and he was weak in health. In discussions where he had usually been a lively participant he would be silent for a time, making no comment. Berggrav seemed to be exhausted.

Amid the widespread expectations for a better future for the Church of Norway, Berggrav did resume his position as Bishop of Oslo. It was not long before he was as active as ever. Kathrine, writing to a friend at the end of May, complained, "I saw more of him when he was imprisoned than I do now!"

The principal Communist publication, *Friheten,* led an attack upon him with several articles throughout June. Other publications and especially the daily papers, *Dagbladet* and *Verdens Gang,* joined in and adopted a critical tone towards the Bishop of Oslo. For some time, Berggrav was the favorite subject for the cartoonist of *Dagbladet* and little by little this criticism became bitter. Not only was Berggrav criticized about his role in the war, but very often the cartoon played on Berggrav's alleged tendency to get into the center of things and push himself forward.

Several incidents gave rise to this, particularly in the spring of 1945 when many thought that he should have held back and been less prominent when Crown Prince Olav returned to the capital. Another incident led to the same impression of Berggrav. When the Rector of Oslo University returned from his imprisonment in Germany and an official welcome was arranged, Berggrav assumed a prominent position and made a speech of welcome—quite spontaneous and certainly not part of the official programme—that outshone all the prepared speeches. What was also remembered by many was that Berggrav and the Rector had been of quite different minds in those April days of 1940.

Such incidents, of course, made this a difficult time for Berggrav, and when the Investigations Commission began its work on the events of 1940, things were no better. Several of his letters and his book, *Da Kampen Kam* (published in 1945), were investigated by the Commission and he was required to report and defend parts of his criticism. The wound was very deep. Ten years later, in 1955, he wrote that he had lost all desire to travel to northern Norway because of the wall of rejection against which he had fought in the summer of 1940.

Not only did a personal burden complicate the situation; Berggrav also had the feeling that behind all this criticism lay a desire to discredit the church. Many indications at that time showed that some actively strove to prevent the further development of the church.

THE BISHOP WITH KID GLOVES

Berggrav was strongly opposed to the death penalty and this gave him the reputation of wanting to treat the criminals of the occupation with "kid gloves." In the first edition of *Kirke og Kultur* after the occupation, Berggrav published a long article (38 pages!) which was also circulated as an offprint and translated into Danish. Its title was "The Judgment of the Nazis by the People from a Human and a Moral Point of View." Many could not agree with him when he wrote that every execution via the death penalty was a failure of the people.

Dagbladet wrote scornfully about "Bishops with kid gloves," but the church also offered opposition. The approval of the death penalty by the conservative theologian Ole Hallesby in his book *Ethics* (published in 1928) was still decisive for many Christians in Norway. Berggrav had stated his firm conviction and held to his word, regardless of what Hallesby had declared. After his meeting with Vidkun Quisling in prison on October 16, 1945, he petitioned the Prime Minister, Einar Gerhardsen, for a reprieval of Quisling's death sentence. In his letter, Berggrav pointed out that his petition was not only on the grounds of his principles, but because he was convinced that it would be an *injustice* if Quisling were executed. He explained that "Among those who knew him and the whole situation best, it appears to be crystal clear that he largely acted in good faith when he had responsibility for these atrocities." Berggrav argued that while the legal process had dealt with the question of guilt, the humanitarian judgment had not yet been given.

By his rejection of the death penalty, Berggrav laid himself open not only to the so-called hard-liners, but in the debate that followed he also provoked the other wing. Part of his argument was that such strong criminal proceedings against all Nazis would make the death penalty excessive. The thought that all members of the Nazi Party during the war years should be punished without any regard to their behavior generated strong reactions on both sides of the question. Berggrav's argument was based upon the principle of "collective guilt," so that even *passive* members of the Nazi Party would be included in the judgment. This argument released a flood of letters from Party Members or their dependants, many of which were anonymous.

From the beginning of 1946, Berggrav was under pressure from people who wanted to see the church take up the question of criminal proceeding and call for reconciliation, in order that the convicted collaborators might regain the confidence of the people.

At the Bishops' Conference in November 1946, Berggrav drafted a letter to the Minister of Justice in which he made a series of critical comments on the way criminal proceedings were being conducted. Such initiatives showed that the church was ready to express views on social ethics that were not necessarily the views of the general population or the authorities. Berggrav's standpoint on the just conviction of collaborators involved him in the administration of justice. This letter gave a clear picture of the nature of the relationship between the power of the church and of the state. For Berggrav, the involvement in human rights issues and his understanding of the role of the church in relation to the state arose from his experience in the occupation years. The church struggle had shown that many things needed to be changed. The opportunity to effect these changes occupied far more of the Bishop's time and energy than answering his critics in these post-war years.

What troubled him most were those embittered Nazi Party members who had chosen Berggrav to be their worst enemy. The main point of their criticism was the statement he had made in the autumn of 1940 concerning the question of Nazi Party membership: that each person should follow his own conviction. (He had seemed to speak in their favor before the war but now opposed to them.) This had also been the critical point of attack in the Communist newspaper, *Friheten.* In the following years those who had been Party Members repeatedly quoted this in their defense. Berggrav pointed out to the pastors that considerable pressure to join the party was being used on them by the Nazis. Berggrav had attempted to say something which could be read carefully between the lines, but for some it was too clever and they clung to the literal meaning of what he said. Berggrav had written in his pastoral letter of October 1940 that every pastor should be free to decide in matters of party membership. He was giving a signal that the pastors should not feel obliged to join the Party, but instead follow their conscience. Of course, the Nazis, not least Quisling himself, used this phrase to show that Berggrav in 1940 had allowed pastors to join his party. They coupled with it the unfortunate episode involving the megaphone in *Krogskogen*. Some attacks on Berggrav were so persistent that, as late as 1949, some who felt they were injured by him wanted to initiate criminal proceedings against him.

A WORN-OUT BISHOP

These many attacks had an injurious effect upon Berggrav's health. He was very ill at Pentecost 1946, shortly after a visit to England to attend the conference of Bible Societies at Elfinsward, a diocesan house under the bishopric of George Bell of Chichester. Berggrav chaired the conference and was later appointed the first President, and here they decided to form the United Bible Societies. The contrast between the attitude towards him in England and in Norway intensified his health trouble. When he returned to Norway, the doctor examined him and found that one of his problems was a weakness of the heart muscles. The doctor blamed his poor condition on stress and psychological pressure. For the following four months, Berggrav was relieved of all his duties and given a period of convalescence that allowed him some time to consider his situation. During this period the bishopric in Hamar fell vacant and Berggrav seriously considered taking the unusual step of leaving Oslo for the position in Hamar. Many in Hamar would have been glad to see Berggrav as their new bishop, but stronger powers ensured that he stayed in Oslo. Several leaders pressed him to stay and even the government joined the appeal, finalizing his need to remain as Bishop of Oslo.

"The government put so much pressure on me," he wrote to a colleague, "that in the end there was nothing else that I could do but stay." The Minister of Religion and Education consulted Berggrav's doctor to see how the bishop could be helped to improve his health. Many steps were taken, including more clerical assistance, longer holidays, and even a partition of the huge diocese of Oslo.

Berggrav now concentrated on bringing more young pastors into the administration of the church and led many young people to become ordained as clergy, preparing the church in Norway for growth. But soon came news from the doctors that he suffered from angina and must take more rest.

The Death of Kathrine

During the years of her husband's incarceration, Kathrine suffered greatly. She had been very active in her work among the wives of the pastors and was most influential in promoting the health of the diocese. Her home was always open. Yet the post-war strain deeply wore on her; she was distressed by the criticism leveled at her husband and alarmed by his deteriorating health. Perhaps in all this she neglected her own health, for she was often active beyond her strength. In April 1947 Kathrine died. Her death was a near-mortal blow to Berggrav. Her commitment was recognized not only in Norway, but throughout Scandinavia and her work and example as a bishop's wife was seen as remarkable. Berggrav could say of her, "I was a man who needed someone to correct him and this was achieved in my life by Kathrine. Only after God and with God, she alone formed and supported me."

In the autumn of 1950, he decided to give up the office of Bishop of Oslo and devote his remaining years to the world church. He twice planned to go to America, but in the summer of 1950, after several small heart attacks, his doctor insisted that he must retire.

THE RETIREMENT

Once he had relinquished the day-to-day business of the bishop's office, he was free to do those things that lay upon his heart, tasks in both Norway and throughout the world. His time as a church leader was not over. He was called upon to advise and was regarded in Norway as a kind of super-bishop without bureaucratic involvement.

One task above all demanded his energy and wisdom: the Ecumenical Movement. He was deeply involved in both the formation of the World Council of Churches and in the cooperation of the national Bible Societies in the United Bible Societies, of which he was first moderator and then President from 1947 until 1957.

A NEW CONSTITUTION
FOR THE CHURCH OF NORWAY

The relationship between church and state had long troubled Berggrav. In the 1930s the relationship was frequently a source of contention. Berggrav argued for the right of the bishops to decide who should be fit to hold the pastoral office and who should be appointed to a specific charge. He saw the interference of the state in these matters as contrary to Lutheran doctrine. The church should govern its own affairs in matters that concern the church without a government's right to veto. This came to a head during the church struggle and, in his cabin under house arrest, Berggrav began work on a new constitution that would support these principles. The results of this work were published in 1945 in a book titled *Kirkens ordning in Norge (The Church Order in Norway)*. The political programme for renewal, *Fellesprogrammet (Common Programme)*, which all parties accepted, had expressed the wish that a new constitutional relationship be worked out between church and state. Beginning with the *Kirkens Grunn (Confession and Declaration)* of Easter 1942, which formed the basis of the church resistance to Quisling, Berggrav developed a fifth section, "The Proper Relationship of Christians and the Church to the Authorities." His book was not simply a personal view. It represented considerable discussion with other bishops and evangelical church leaders. Its spirit was that of the last words of the *Kirkens Grunn:* "The Evangelical Lutheran Church is today, as it was to the generations before us, our spiritual Fatherland in Norway." Three years later it was clear, in a liberated Norway, that much work needed to be done to define the church-state relationship in view of the experience of a Nazi-imposed relationship.

On November 23, 1945, by a decision of the King, a Commission was set up to prepare a new church constitution for Norway. Berggrav was appointed chairman of this Commission and its membership was drawn from various sections of the church. Ole Hallesby was an influential member, a former Minister of Religion and Education in the Social Democratic Party was included, as well as theologians of various emphases. The Commission held out no guarantees that the members would always agree with Berggrav. In fact, it was free to propose suggestions that were very different from those in his book of 1945.

Berggrav was opposed to a democratic ruling of the church. He placed an authority on the views of those ordained and emphasized the role of personalities. The church had its own principle of leadership, based upon a "spiritual fellowship." This thought, above all, raised strong opposition from the laity and the old church reformers.

The Commission presented its recommendations. Among other proposals, it suggested a national council or synod, composed of 23 members, of whom 13 were lay people. Only three bishops were proposed to sit on the council, although Berggrav wanted seven. Some three years later, this issued in a draft law for parliament, but Berggrav was not satisfied. In 1951, he sent a long letter to the leading members of the Commission suggesting that this new church organization be further discussed and meanwhile be put on hold: "The main problem here is the bureaucracy ... perhaps also the welfare state," he said. He characterized the draft law as a "nanny system." Despite his strong views, he did not want a public debate. He was prepared to leave the matter to be taken up by the voluntary church meetings. He wrote that in political circles this would be called an abuse of power. He could foresee that the political climate was changing.

These fears were not groundless. Beginning with the handling of the government draft in 1953, the attacks on the church became more and more severe. The worst came from members of the Labor Party who had strongly criticized Berggrav's *Kirkens ordning*. Berggrav recognized that any proposal made on one of his ideas, with too brief an explanation, could cause a strong reaction. He was particularly disappointed that the radicals in the Labor Party had changed their attitude. In fact there was no clear line in parliament—even a section of the Social Democrats voted against their own government! This parliamentary debate began in the early months of 1953. The various church organizations also engaged in considerable debate, often quite bitter, including talk of broken promises and of bourgeois politicians stopping up the wells of criticism. The radical members of the Labor Party put forward points of view with which Berggrav had great difficulty in agreeing. He had not avoided the great debate—even the church struggle was used as an argument to curtail the influence of the church.

Berggrav himself belonged to those who were critical of the changing course in the parliamentary debate. Thus, when the "Voluntary Church Council" sent a letter to the parliament in the new year (1953), Berggrav added to it a letter of his own. He took the majority of the Committee to task for their suggestion that the church had had a taste of power and now wished to hold on to it. He denied the lust for power of which the church was accused: "In this matter, the church has laid before the state with great clarity that it is the church's right to account for the interest of the people and in the cause of truth, in matters concerning the church, as is allowed by our democratic system and the biblical teaching of the Christian church."

In the parliamentary voting, the government suffered a defeat and in the closing debate, the proposal for the church to have its own Council was lost.

In spite of this, Berggrav was unusually careful in his comments. He was aware that strong reactions from the side of the church would weaken the standing of the church among the people. The situation presented him with a dilemma: on the one hand, he very much wanted the church to have an independent standing with regard to the state; on the other hand, he lay great emphasis on the value of the church still being a state church, with tolerance and with meaningful influence. In the *Kirkens ordning*, he had written: "The church of this land should become a church for the people, not against the people."

THE LABOR PARTY AND THE WELFARE STATE

Despite the situation, Berggrav saw a gleam of light in that the Labor Party no longer presented a united front against the church. In the years that followed the war, Berggrav sought systematically to build up close relations with the center of the Labor Party in a trustful relationship, with the hope that the unhappy hostility between church and Labor Party might be overcome. The cooperation between representatives of the church and leaders of the resistance movement, as well as the work on the "United Programme" of the coalition government, had created a better climate and a greater openness.

In the years that followed, Berggrav used every opportunity to raise the question of relations between the church and the Labor Movement both openly and in private conversations with leading members of the Labor Party. Berggrav had established a good relationship on a personal and trusting basis with the Labor Prime Minister, Einar Gerhardsen. He respected the Prime Minister as a man; he described him as a "politician with a warm heart," for whom the human dimension held first place.

In the Oslo Bishop's Annual Report for 1948, he wrote quite frankly about the relationship of the church to the Labor Party. He could register voices in the Labor Party that were antagonistic to Christianity, but declared that the majority of its members were more positive in their attitude to the church.

The problem resided with certain key figures, propagandists, and literary men who presented a different profile of the church. Berggrav could find no evidence for a consistent attitude to the church in the Party. Some changes in opinions about the Labor Party were also brewing in the church. A growing consciousness of social problems in Christian circles led to sympathy for the social warmth of the Labor Party. Berggrav found himself critical of the Labor Party as well as of the church.

But Berggrav remained especially critical of the Party on one point. They had always followed a reductionist line in relation to the church and Christianity, weakening the position of religious education and undermining Christian values concerning the family, marriage, and sexual morality.

In 1948, Parliament made a decision to supply contraceptives to all Norwegian soldiers in the German Brigade, a detachment involved in the occupation of Germany. Berggrav clearly disapproved of this, as did many Norwegian citizens. An initiative was taken to send a "Letter from the People" to the Norwegian Parliament, for which 450,000 signatures were collected. Berggrav was one of those who gave this document with its signatures to the President of the Parliament.

Berggrav's objective was to achieve a situation in which the church and the Party, working together on concrete issues, presented no problem for Christians to vote for the Labor

Party. In this letter he showed clearly the influence of the Christian Socialist Movement with which he had become acquainted in England, not least from William Temple, formerly Archbishop of Canterbury. Of course, he had to make clear that the church could in no way identify itself with any one political party. But what had for so long been difficult for Christians, namely to vote Socialist, could possibly no longer be a problem. His words were carefully chosen: "Our task as Christians is not to embrace a socialistic political party, but to work with it in such a way that the social atmosphere becomes so fruitful and so warm that it corresponds to the will of God. Then we would be ready to help achieve that goal."

Berggrav had no interest in a Christian political party, which he regarded as an unnatural combination of confession of faith and party loyalty. But he saw that the church could work with a political party, if the importance of Christianity in all parts of social life was recognized and its validity and influence would not be reduced to a narrow sector of life. He insisted that the freedom of a Christian to obey the will of God be maintained in society.

Berggrav was skeptical of any attempt to establish a Christian party, yet he sought conditions for an alliance between the church and the ruling Labor Party. In this he was consciously forming a strategy for a better church constitution. Contacts between church leaders and prominent members of the Labor Party inevitably led to a better understanding. This policy caused strong tensions in the Party, where many were very skeptical about the church.

It is possible that Berggrav himself added to this skepticism in 1952 when he addressed the Lutheran World Federation, meeting in Hannover that summer. The theme of his address was to be the relationship between the church and the modern state. His views were well-known and nothing very controversial was expected. In 1948, he had spoken optimistically about this relationship. He saw no major problems. But by 1952, things had changed. His earlier problem-free attitudes to the modern state were known in England and Germany through his book on the state and the individual. Now, preparing this address some years later, he wrote to the General Secretary of the Lutheran World Federation, Carl E. Lundquist, "I had not realized how much the situation had changed and how many more difficult questions had arisen in these few years." He toiled at this address, rewriting and rewriting his manuscript five times. And even then he was dissatisfied with it. At last, he told Lundquist that it was ready, but complained that unfortunately, it was not good.

Despite all his hesitations, Berggrav delivered his lecture, "Church and State Today from a Lutheran Point of View."

The address had two main parts. In the first part, he dealt with the classical problems of the limits to obedience to the state. Here he developed the thoughts that he had expressed in a well-known address during the war years: "When the Driver is Drunk." There he attacked the Lutheran church which had so often guaranteed the legitimacy of the *status quo*. Strong statements had been made by Lutheran theologians about absolute obedience even to a tyrannical authority. He went on to show how Romans 13 had been misused in the history of the church.

Berggrav's understanding of Paul consisted in recognizing that the central idea of the duty of obedience was based upon justice and not upon power. If the state deals with its citizens unjustly, a situation can arise in which it is not only permissible, but in fact a duty, to take an attitude of active resistance to the state.

Naturally, Berggrav's point of view did not go unchallenged among the German Lutherans. His thesis on the right to revolution unleashed a long-lasting debate. In 1956, a symposium was published in Berlin on *Macht und Recht (Might and Right)* in which several Lutheran theologians and lawyers took up Berggrav's thesis and analyzed it. Many of them had to admit that the Norwegian bishop touched upon a sore point of Lutheran theology.

But the second part of his address also set an intensive debate in motion. The problem, he stated, was the relationship between the church and the modern welfare state, a theme he had had the most difficulty preparing in the manuscript. During his earlier work, "The State and the Individual," he was unable to find a collective term for the tendency of the state to take over more and more responsibility for social life, a tendency he criticized. Now in 1952, the term "welfare state" seemed to be the term he sought to express the tendency he criticized. It had become the hallmark of progressive states after the war.

Berggrav feared that despite its secular character, the welfare state took precedence over all other organizations in society and entered into—perhaps controlled—every aspect of life. That led to an uneven balance between the two realms church and state. The new state took such a grasp of the spiritual realm that the church was driven out of many aspects of social life. In this scenario Christianity became a private practice, while the welfare state with its insertion into every area of life became a kind of "almighty" spiritual structure.

Berggrav was not alone in his concern about what would happen in a welfare state where so many things that had been the concern of the churches and voluntary organizations were taken over. About the same time Berggrav was giving his address to the LWF, Emil Brunner, a distinguished theologian from Zürich, was speaking at the annual meeting of the Free Church Federal Council in Cardiff, Wales. He faced representatives of the Methodist Conference, knowing that they had worked over many years for the welfare state with compassion for the underprivileged. Brunner said, "Well, you now have the welfare state for which you have worked so long. The question now is, 'What will you do with it?'" What the churches of Europe had done over the centuries with hospitals, social centers, homes for elderly people, and many other services to those in need was "up for grabs" when the state "nationalized" the welfare system and spoke of caring for the people "from the cradle to the grave." Inevitably, some of the well-established welfare organizations of the churches went out of business or were taken over by the state. In some countries, including Britain, people welcomed the new responsibilities assumed by the government. Research was undertaken on the needs of those who fell through the net. Berggrav saw more clearly than most the effect this might have, namely, reducing the work of the church to its own buildings, privatizing the church. But it was not only his concern for the effects on the church. With such far-reaching welfare work, the state was in danger of becoming totalitarian. His skepticism was not always well received in Germany or Norway. The Labor Party saw in his warnings a move to strengthen the role of the church in public affairs. The warm relationship that he had built up with leaders of the Labor Party began to cool. In the controversies that followed, Berggrav went further, warning of the danger of the individual citizen becoming a number in statistical surveys until he or she was anonymous. He also saw the danger of a welfare state weakening individual initiative.

In 1957, when the Labor Party launched its Programme, Berggrav was soon in the debate, claiming that the Programme assumed a much more optimistic faith in humankind! He also detected in the Programme a humanistic and non-religious view of life. For this reason he opposed the taking over of some religious institutions by the state, particularly hospitals, clinics, and schools.

Already in the address to the LWF in 1952, he claimed that religious freedom meant more than freedom to preach the Word of God but included "the right to show to the people the need for a proper use of wealth and the exercise of compassion." Strong interference from the state in these areas left the church "socially impotent," he said, and he urged resistance to such political activities.

10

Church, State, and the Doctrine of Unity

Although Eivind Berggrav was criticized in Norway, he was a hero on the international scene. The many international organizations coming to birth after the war sought his involvement and endorsement. In church and state, particularly in Britain and America, he was regarded as the Norwegian *Bishop of the Resistance.*

Norway is predominantly Lutheran. Other denominations there, which are of considerable size in England and the United States, are small minorities. Even the Roman Catholic Church has little influence in the land. The Lutheran Church of Norway has legal status. The government has influence over the church and is responsible for its finances and much of its administration. This inevitably raises questions of the separate responsibilities of church and state. For a very long time, Berggrav had been concerned about the freedom of the church to manage its own affairs without breaking the church-state relationship.

Another factor in the religious life of Norway is the existence of pietistic groups, who plan and execute mission work in Norway and overseas. They are sometimes hostile to the incumbent of a parish, but are dependent upon their local church for the sacraments. Otherwise, they arrange their own worship and religious teaching. Two of the strongest of these are the Inner Mission and the China Mission. The latter was renamed *Norsk Luthersk Misjonssamband* (The Norwegian Lutheran Missionary Society) in 1948, but ten years later it was still called *Kinamisjon* in popular parlance. Many societies are enthusiastic and their meetings are well attended. As they raise their funds on a voluntary basis, they are often quite well financed. They present a problem to the parish church, which Berggrav recognized early in his ministry.

The war period offered a temporary solution to both these problems.

When Quisling assumed an illegitimate authority over the church, the break between church and state was immediate. The Church of Norway became, temporarily, like a Free Church in England. It managed its own affairs and refused to submit to the state, because it was not recognized as a legitimate government.

The resistance to the puppet government of Quisling brought the Church of Norway and the Inner Mission together with other religious communities to a form of cooperative relationship, made possible by the mutual respect and trust that Eivind Berggrav and Ole Hallesby had for each other. The opposition to the Quisling government was stronger than their differences. Together they began to work on a new constitution for the church. As in most occupied countries, the end of the war loosened the bonds that had held disparate parties together. The common enemy was gone.

In the 1950s, Berggrav's energies went into dealing with these two issues: church and state; and church and religious communities (or prayer houses). A related problem was the question of preserving the basic doctrines of the church. A Lutheran Church has its prime authority in the Bible, but a close second is the Confessions or more precisely the Lutheran

Evangelical Confessions. These doctrinal statements were written at the time of the Reformation and were normative for the Lutheran churches that emerged from the conflict with Rome. Berggrav was also aware that the bond, which had held during the occupation between church and people, was also weakened in peacetime.

THE RIGHTS OF THE CHURCH AND THE AUTHORITY OF THE STATE

In 1928, when the Minister of Religious Affairs refused to ratify the appointment of the liberal theologian, Kristian Schjelderup, to a vacant parish, he was within his rights. Berggrav recognized this and supported the action. There was an outcry among the liberals and Berggrav sympathized with it. But the Constitution allowed the state that power. He did not protest against the action, but wrote an article criticizing the Constitution. He argued that a revision of the Constitution was needed. "The bishops and not the government should be the guardians of the door into the church," he maintained. This also applied to ordination of clergy, which he said should be solely the decision of the church.

The extreme action taken by the church during the occupation was possible because Quisling's government was illegitimate. It was an issue of rebellion, permitted by Luther, against a tyrannical government. The action was extreme: the resignation, first of bishops, then of clergy, and all that this involved.

At the end of the war, the situation changed and the state returned more or less to the *status quo*. Yet work on a new constitution of the church had begun, giving the church much more self-control. But documents and laws never settle issues until there is a case to be judged.

The case came when a distinguished lawyer intervened in the debate over hell. The issue was whether Schjelderup's statement that there is no place for hell in a religion of love disqualified him from his pastoral oversight of a Lutheran church.

Berggrav took the line of attempting reconciliation, claiming that the matter involved the church and should be regarded as a dispute between orthodoxy and liberal theology, or the parish church and the Inner Mission.

Professor Frede Castberg, the distinguished lawyer, supported by the Ministry of Religion and Education, ruled that Article 2 in the Church Constitution (that dealing with the requirements of the clergy to accept the Confessions) should be taken in a general sense, interpreted broadly, and that Schjelderup had said nothing against the overall content of the Confessions. This intervention greatly irritated Berggrav because he believed that such a ruling could only be made by the church. In his justification of the ruling, Castberg wrote that while the church had a spiritual authority, it had no consequences in law. Berggrav responded with an article, "Contra Castberg," with the subtitle *"Om kirkens grunn"* ("Concerning the Church's Constitution"). He argued that if Castberg's reasoning had been accepted during the occupation there would have been no resistance and no church struggle. Castberg had argued that the church should never resist the law or make difficulties, even when the state interferes with its internal affairs. Berggrav responded that the spiritual and the legal have equal authority in their own sphere. The church requires a protective outer structure, which the state can provide, but its purpose is to preserve the spiritual identity of the church, not to control or direct it. There is no mistaking Berggrav's irritation at the way Castberg had taken upon himself, as a lawyer and representative of the state, to interpret the Confessions. A legal ruling or a government decision on the Confessions should be the prerogative of the church itself. He had described Quisling's illegitimate assumption of authority over the church as "a blow struck at the altar," and this was incorporated in the Confessional document *Kirkens grunn*. Now he used the same argument against Castberg. He spoke quite plainly, accusing the state of acting as though it had the authority of a Pope. "In these matters," Berggrav said quite categorically, "the church leaders cannot trust the judgment of the politicians."

LEARNING FROM THE AMERICAN CHURCHES

In the summer and autumn of 1954, Berggrav spent almost six months in the United States. Many of the things that he had desired for his own church he saw realized in American churches. Writing about his visit in *Kirke og Kultur,* he described the American examples of church life that inspired his thinking about the future of the church in Norway. First he mentioned the strong social function of the church, that it seemed to be at the center of all human life and embraced a much wider sphere of interest than it did in Europe. He thought that the American churches fulfilled the church's calling better than in any other country, nurturing a relationship with God in Christ and better relationships among human beings, especially among Christians. The visit gave him many fruitful opportunities to reconsider his plans for the church in Norway. "The Norwegians suffer under the mistaken view," he said, "that laboring in the Lord's vineyard is confined to preaching or service in hospitals.... We must give ourselves to more than that.... We must involve ourselves in a greater variety of activities, tasks that serve the human race in health and in sickness."

When he made his visit to the United States, he was already well known to many American church leaders, especially those who, like him, had seen the need for a closer relationship between the churches throughout the world. As early as 1946 he was in Geneva and preached in services with Martin Niemöller of Germany and Dr. Chester Miao of China. In 1948, he had taken a prominent part in the Amsterdam Assembly. It was natural, therefore, that he should be in America for the Second Assembly of the World Council of Churches in Evanston on the theme of Christian Hope.

He spent six months as an honored guest of the American churches and a friend of many of its leaders. He had ample opportunity to study the vitality of the churches and to recognize in their expansion the Spirit that moved him all his life. He saw the idea of "crossing frontiers" in action on a large scale. The frontier was the symbol of America; it was the character of it churches. No longer geographical, the frontier had been discovered in the minds of Christian Americans. They were forever discovering new fields of Christian discipleship. As Berggrav made these discoveries, they quickened his own tendency to want to cross frontiers.

By the 1950s, Berggrav, now in his 70s, was still full of life and ready to take on new ideas and new methods. He had a respect for the traditional values, but his vision included new forms of worship and specific tasks for the church. At the center of his thinking stood the solid tradition, so that amid the changes and decay in the life of the church he was able to move with confidence into new territories of thought and action. In 1954, inspired by what he saw in America, he spoke often about building a stronger relationship between the church and the cultural life of the nation. Nevertheless, he insisted that this was *not* his main purpose. In his words, "The church can establish no cultural program before it has realized its Christian program."

BERGGRAV AND THE ROYAL HOUSE

The traditional side of Berggrav's character was never more clearly expressed than in his admiration of the monarchy. In 1930, he wrote that the monarchy fulfilled—in a special way—the needs of the people for something unchanging. Amid all the changes of life, the monarchy represented something solid and unifying which satisfied a natural psychological need and provided a stabilizing structure in society. At that time, ten years before the German invasion, Berggrav observed and noted publicly that a monarch who is united in solidarity of mind and heart with his people is vitally important for Norway.

Behind his theories on such a figure in society lay his deep personal respect for King Haakon VII, who had reigned over Norway since 1905. He expressed this view at the time of the Olav Celebrations in 1930, but it was confirmed often during the war years. Every year, during the annual dinner at the Bishops' Conference, the King was invited to address the assembly and this gave church leaders an opportunity to raise questions about the church. But more important still were the personal contacts and the King's own interest in religious matters, affecting the spiritual health of his people. King Haakon expressed a particular interest in the Oxford Group movement. This movement was popular in Scandinavia, because it seemed to offer a healthy alternative to the permissiveness that World War I had brought about even in neutral countries. By 1938, its name had changed to "Moral Rearmament." It had global influence, but gradually died out. It persisted in Scandinavia longer than in other parts of the world. The interest of the King, and also of Berggrav, was in its power to commit young people to higher moral standards.

In the years that followed World War II, "Moral Rearmament" exercised a fascination for several politicians and statesmen in Europe, as well as leaders in some of the Colonies. The movement had a house in Caux, above Montreux, in Switzerland, where leaders from many countries were invited to come and stay with others from whom they had been estranged: representatives of Colonial Powers and leaders of independent movements in their Colonies, Germans and Italians with those who had so recently fought against them, and others. Their theory was that if they lived and ate together for a week or so in relaxed surroundings, they would become reconciled. It was a bold experiment and clearly the world needed "moral rearmament" after so much destruction.

It was not surprising that Berggrav and the King were interested in a movement that embodied what they both desired: peace and reconciliation. Together they showed some interest also in a play that was touring round the world: *The Forgotten Factor.* The movement attracted many famous people in the field of sport and the arts, as well as political leaders. This would most certainly be among the topics discussed at the dinner of the Conference of Bishops in these years.

But in addition to the contacts at the Conference of Bishops and the shared interests of King and Bishop, an important relationship continued between them at a deeply personal level. Queen Maud was in England during the autumn of 1938 and fell seriously ill. When Berggrav heard of her illness, he went at once to attend her. The journey was made at his initiative, but on his arrival the queen was already dead. All he could do was to accompany the body back to Oslo via Portsmouth. Once in Oslo, he gave a radio talk with the title, "The Last Journey of the Queen." The talk showed his strong sense of loyalty, not only to the Queen, but also to the whole royal household. Berggrav was criticized in the newspapers for this submissiveness, giving the impression to many people that there was something more in his admiration than what appeared. But the King was delighted with his involvement, as were the Crown Prince Olav and his wife, Princess Martha.

During the years of his imprisonment, Berggrav was able to keep in touch with his King and the exiled government in England. It was, in fact, on the King's advice that he refused the offer of rescue, escape, and exile, even though he would have been glad to be with King Haakon during those war years.

The relationship of Berggrav with the Crown Prince Olav and his wife went back to 1934, when they visited North Norway where Berggrav was the Bishop of Hålogaland. He was naturally much involved in arranging their visit and making sure they enjoyed and learned from the people. The Princess published a life of Queen Maud, a book of photographs to which Berggrav wrote the text. His own biography of the Queen was written two years later in 1956, entitled *Mennesket Dronning Maud (A Very Human Queen).*

On March 21, 1954, the Crown Prince and his Princess celebrated their silver wedding under very extraordinary circumstances. Princess Martha was seriously ill in hospital. A service of celebration was held in the Royal Palace Chapel, in which the royal family took part. Although no longer Bishop of Oslo, Berggrav was invited to preach the sermon. He preached on Paul's great song of love (1 Corinthians 13). To the congregation his words were unforgettable:

> Love on this earth is God's next door neighbor, between them there is scarcely any wall. And because of this, love can be renewed from the deepest wells and is never without hope, because it lives so near to forgiveness.

Berggrav also developed a good relationship with the younger generation of the royal house. In his official duties as bishop he was in close contact with the children of the Crown Prince, instructing all in preparation for their confirmation. He described his time in 1947 with the young princesses, Ragnhild and Astrid, as "moments of joy in a difficult time of criticism and accusations." Six years later when it was time for Prince Harold to be confirmed, he instructed him also.

THE CORONATION OF KING OLAV

In 1957, King Haakon died and was succeeded by the Crown Prince Olav. The new king wished to decide upon the type of coronation service he should have. As early as 1949, Berggrav had prepared a liturgy for such an occasion. Olav chose this service and asked that it be held in the ancient Nidaros Cathedral in Trondheim, conducted by two bishops, Johannes Smemo and Arne Fjellbu; the preacher was Eivind Berggrav, although he was no longer in office. This coronation sermon revealed a great deal about Berggrav's attitude to the monarchy.

Berggrav's support for the monarchy was not only his general sympathy for one form of traditional constitution, but even more to be understood in the light of his views on the church. He persisted in working for a church that belonged to the people—a national church, a people's church—all that is meant by the European concept of a *Volkskirche*. The celebration of the coronation in Nidaros Cathedral brought King, church, and people closer together, just as Berggrav had always wanted. His contribution as church leader in the post war years can be seen largely as an attempt to validate the *Volkskirche* tradition in the church and at the same time to win back to the church those whom it had lost.

In 1950, he had spoken on the radio about the church in the first half of the 20th century. Looking back over those 50 years, he said, the church had lived through a "period of strife, work, and growing up, maturing." Yet the most important lesson that he had learned from this survey of the years was that the church can never stand still and can never give up learning new things. His characteristic last sentence was, "The church is in no way *'ferdig,'* in every sense of that word." (*Ferdig* is a word that combines being *ready* and *completed*.) His use of the word, and especially his deliberate pointing to the double meaning of that word, enabled him to say that the church was neither ready for the tasks that lay ahead of it nor finished in its growth towards maturity.

THE PREACHER

In his account of Berggrav's significant role in the formation of the World Council of Churches, Alex Johnson writes, "Berggrav was not only a valuable committee member in the work of the World Council of Churches, but he was above all, a preacher." And he gives as an example of this, the sermon he preached at the Opening Service of the Oslo World Student Conference in 1947. It was held in the cathedral, which at that time was still under repair with a false roof, while the vault above was being restored. 1400 young people from 80 nations listened in silence as he preached on "The World Kingdom of

God." He drew attention to the false roof and compared it to our waiting for the rule of God over the world. The false roof lies heavy over us all, because the artist must have somewhere to stand while he paints the true vault. We do not yet see the vault, because the artist has not yet finished his work. But we wait until the false roof is taken away and a marvelous view will appear to feast our eyes. This is how God deals with history. We suffer now under the pressure of the low roof, which many times he lays upon us. We should know, however, that he only does it that we might one day see the vault in its glorious completion.

Berggrav was not only good at drawing upon his surroundings for illustration, but also ready to use even mishaps during his conduct of worship. On that occasion in Oslo, when his sermon was ended and he moved down from the pulpit to the altar to give the blessing, a misunderstanding with the organist occurred. Berggrav began, somewhat quietly, with the explanation, "If I may, I will give the blessing in Norwegian." The organist did not hear, and assumed it as the usual greeting: "The Lord be with you," and played for the congregational response, "And with thy spirit." As Berggrav then said, "The Lord be with you," the organist thought it was the blessing, and thundered out the threefold "Amen," followed with his usual piece after the blessing, going on for some time. Berggrav stood quite still until the organ was silent. Then he finally said in a loud voice and this time in English, "So is it often in life that one has to wait for God's blessing, but it always comes." And now it came in Berggrav's voice and went straight to the hearts of all present.

Alex Johnson also tells of an incident that happened almost twenty years before which shows the same man, always alert to turn mishaps into blessings. At a wedding in 1928, the bridegroom had been ill and asked if instead of standing during the ceremony they could both sit on chairs before the altar, Berggrav agreed, but the verger did not remember and was, in any case, rather nervous.

At the point where the couple was about to sit, the verger pulled away the bride's chair and she fell to the ground. She was quickly on her feet again. Berggrav was quite undisturbed, but in a quiet voice addressed the bride before proceeding, saying as though it were part of the ritual: "When the saintly King Olav first landed on the Norwegian coast, he slipped and fell. Then Rane, the king's tutor, said, 'Your Majesty, now you have taken hold of this land.' So it is with you, Elizabeth, now you have taken hold of this land into which you are entering. And this fall of yours will give to you health and happiness."

Amid all his sorrows, responsibilities, and struggles for the church, the state, the Royal House, and the unity of the faith, Eivind Berggrav remained a profoundly caring servant of Christ.

11

Churches in the World

The 20th century has seen the most significant move in history to foster dialogue and cooperation between church bodies around the world. Initial efforts began with a missionary conference in Edinburgh, a gathering that sought to reduce conflict between missionaries in Asia and Africa. It led, especially in America, to a movement bringing together the churches for peace in the world. From this, the Life and Work movement arose. At the same time, the churches felt the need to understand one another and simplify the complex organizations caused by a divided church. The representation of the Gospel to a pagan world would be more effective if proclaimed by a unified church. The words of Jesus in his prayer in John 17 called for the church to be one "that the world may believe."

This impulse to bring the churches together was given the unloved name of the Ecumenical Movement. The word "ecumenical" comes from the Greek word *oikumene,* which means "the whole inhabited world." This should have pleased the Evangelicals, fond of singing;

> Christ for the world! We sing;
> The world to Christ we bring
> With loving zeal.

Somehow, the word "ecumenical" did not always give that impression. Berggrav, however, was prepared to wait. When others complained about this odd word, he said: "Two hundred years ago, the word 'mission' sounded strange, nobody had heard it before. So it will be with the word 'ecumenical.' It sounds strange now, but in time it will be accepted as readily as 'mission.' "

A COMMITMENT TO UNITY

Despite the many lessons Berggrav learned during his incarceration and under the influence of the church struggle, it would be wrong to think of that period as the beginning of his involvement in the ecumenical idea. His entire life led him in an ecumenical direction. Already as a student, he met the World Student Christian Federation and felt the inspiration of ecumenical leaders such as John R. Mott. Some years later, his contacts with Nathan Söderblom inaugurated him into the movement. Although Visser't Hooft had early suspicions of Berggrav, he later spoke of him as Nathan Söderblom's successor. His role as ecumenical leader in Scandinavia was recognized.

With some hesitations, Berggrav had allowed himself to be persuaded to become active in the ecumenical organization called the "World Alliance of the Churches for Promoting International Friendship." At a 1938 congress in Larvik, Sigmund-Schulze, whom Berggrav met during World War I while visiting Germany as a war correspondent, persuaded the Bishop of Olso to take an active part in this organization. Together with the General Secretary of the Alliance, H. L. Henriod, Sigmund-Schulze tried to get Berggrav elected President. Despite his reservations Berggrav from that point forward became the "strong man" in this World Alliance; he became Vice-President and the Chairman of the newly appointed

Executive Committee. The last years of this decade were called the "Berggrav era" within the World Alliance, both regionally and internationally.

The work in the World Alliance was directed towards practical actions on behalf of the world and local conditions. He was, for example, more interested in the Stockholm Conference on Life and Work in 1925 than in the Oxford Conference on Faith and Order in 1937. But, by the end of the 1930s he was Chairman of the Norwegian branches of all three ecumenical organizations: World Alliance, Faith and Order, and Life and Work.

During the war years contact with the Ecumenical Movement was inevitably weakened. Eivind Berggrav's best information came from the ecumenical institute in Sigtuna, Sweden, through reports smuggled into his cabin. From time to time news and greetings came to him by various means. In 1944, Kathrine wrote to Henriod asking him to send some crumbs of information about the Ecumenical Movement from Geneva to the lonely prisoner. The isolation was not total and it was surprising how well informed about the development of the Ecumenical Movement Berggrav was when he emerged in 1945. During those years of incarceration, his concern for the unity of the church grew.

In August 1945, Eivind Berggrav received a letter by normal post—his first in five years!—from Visser't Hooft in Geneva. He thanked Berggrav for his involvement during the war and invited him to join the planned Provisional Committee, whose first full meeting would be February 20, 1946, in the Swiss capital.

THE PROVISIONAL COMMITTEE

The decision taken before the war to form a World Council of Churches was revived as soon as possible after peace was established. In February 1946, the process of forming the Council was started at a meeting in Geneva of the Provisional Committee formed for that purpose. On February 20, Berggrav spoke to the Committee, together with Martin Niemöller, who had spent eight years in Hitler's prison. Chester Miao, a prisoner in China, was also present. The congregation wanted to hear of his heroic endurance, but he disappointed them. He said at once, "Don't concern yourself with what we have gone through and don't describe us as heroic. That would not be right." For this reason, Berggrav said nothing about the courage of the church struggle, but simply bore witness to the fact that he and the whole Norwegian church had been taught a lesson, by their isolation, in the reality of ecumenical affairs. "For the first time," he confided, "we in Norway have learnt what 'ecumenical' means; it means the living bonds within us that bind together Christians throughout the world." He explained how this discovery came about: "In concrete terms, this Christian fellowship was shown in the care-packets that came to us. While we were locked up between the walls of our occupation, we knew that many hearts beat for us, in England and America, in Sweden and Denmark and here in Geneva."

He quoted from a letter, which had reached him during the war from Geneva: "Be of good courage. Friends in the worldwide church give thanks and pray also for the Norwegians." Berggrav also gave a further example of what the ecumenical fellowship meant to him during the war. It concerned an episode during his time of house arrest. A neighbor woman came to his kitchen window with a bottle of milk and whispered to him what her husband had heard on the radio: "The Archbishop of Canterbury prayed for you!" He told this story often, with slight variations of emphasis. It obviously meant a great deal to him in his loneliness that the church throughout the world was at prayer and that he and Norway were not forgotten in its prayers. This was for him the essence of the Ecumenical Movement.

The Burge Memorial Lecture

Berggrav was invited to give the Burge Memorial Lecture, a prestigious annual lecture, in King's College, London. He chose as his subject "The Norwegian Church in its International Setting," and addressed the assembly on April 30, 1946. Berggrav used this theme to reflect upon the ecumenical aspect of the Norwegian church struggle. He outlined three elements that remained characteristic of his ecumenical involvement after the war.

1. The struggle for law and justice is a legitimate matter of concern in the ecumenical life of the church. Law as a divine ordinance is an international issue—an *ecumenical* issue. The churches are required to work for the supremacy of law in the international community.

2. The war had taught the value of the Confessions of the church and led the Norwegians to reflect upon their Lutheran tradition. Berggrav saw no contradiction in holding a strong confessional belief and working within the Ecumenical Movement.

3. The Christian fellowship stretches across all human barriers and Christian hope is expressed amid the deprivation and hopelessness shown by the world.

These three were not only points in a lecture, but guidelines for Berggrav's ecumenical involvement. A considerable part of his involvement after the war had to do with international questions and human rights.

His own ecumenical standpoint was not to abolish confessions or denominations for the sake of unity. He was opposed to those who tried to force this through a kind of unity without regard to truth. For him, the unity of the church required more than bureaucratic tidying up.

His ecumenical work did not proceed from the outward, organizational level, but from the existing unity and the fellowship of belief, which stretched out beyond all national, social, and cultural bounds. In his ecumenical thinking, the personal was more important than the institutional.

A week after the Burge Lecture, Berggrav was chairing a meeting in one of the diocesan houses of George Bell's Chichester Diocese, Elfinsward, near Haywards Heath, Sussex, England, which was a conference of Bible Societies. This group was looking at the tasks facing the post-war world in Europe and, as it turned out, predominantly in Germany.

It is easy to detect the common task of George Bell the Anglican and Eivind Berggrav the Lutheran, both of whom labored for peace before and even during the war, both pioneers for unity, while holding fast to their own particular inheritance. These two represented the determination of the post-war churches to stay together. They were men of integrity; they were not redesigners of structures, but men of God.

CONCRETE ACTION

Berggrav's pivotal role in the months following the meeting in Elfinsward led to the formation of the United Bible Societies. At the same time he was much involved in the preparations for the Inaugural Assembly of the World Council of Churches which met eventually in Amsterdam, August 22, 1948. It had been long awaited and the waiting time was not easy. The World Council of Churches had been in process of formation for ten years. The General Secretary, Visser't Hooft, admitted that living between the times had created uncertainties. Should they wait or devise programs without the authority of the churches? With Berggrav on the Provisional Committee, there could be no question of waiting! Visser't Hooft expressed this most clearly when he reported that during the times between existence and non-existence of the Council, the universal church—all those who are God's holy people in Christ—was real and living. "It *happened*," he said "in the testimony of Confessing churches speaking on behalf of the church of Christ as a whole; in the intercession for persecuted churches; in worship services among prisoners of war and refugees; in fraternal aid given to suffering churches and orphaned missions; in relationships restored in the name of the common faith as in Stuttgart and Oslo." The reference to Stuttgart referred to the meeting in the partially ruined Bible House in Stuttgart, October 1945, when representatives of the World Council met German church leaders and heard their confession of guilt, the Stuttgart *Schuldeklärung,* which restored the relationships broken by war. The reference to Oslo was to the Second World Conference of Christian Youth, which helped a new generation of Christians to build together across the divisions caused by war. This kind of work greatly appealed to Berggrav, but he saw the need for practical action once he was involved in the Provisional Committee. That was soon recognized and his role quickly discovered.

When Berggrav spoke of "concrete ecumenical work," the Committee asked him what he meant. At once he drafted a memo and sent it to Geneva. He saw the principal task to be a survey of the churches most damaged by the war, followed by an attempt to restore them. Undoubtedly, he was much influenced by the terrible destruction of the churches in Northern Norway. He had already raised money in Britain for a "church boat" to be used in Finnmark, but now he turned to the Netherlands. In the autumn of 1945 he learned that the Germans had melted down 1200 church bells in the Netherlands for war purposes, giving him an idea for his first ecumenical task. He wrote to all the Norwegian church boards and asked for a gift of 20 kroners each, for the bells of the Netherlands. He raised 20,000 kroners, enough to pay for four new bells and a contribution towards a fifth. He also found a Norwegian company to transport the bells *gratis* to the Netherlands and was himself present for the presentation of each in 1947. They were installed in five Lutheran churches in Schiedam, Nijmegen, Arnhem, Hilversum, and the Martin Luther Church in Amsterdam. Berggrav traveled in the lorry with the bells from church to church and in each congregation he delivered a short speech in his best Dutch! He was a hands-on man.

ATTITUDE TO GERMANY

Considering his close relations with Germany, it came as a surprise that Berggrav was not included in the World Council delegation to receive the Declaration of Guilt from the German church leaders. He did not think it was wise to go, in particular because he was already suffering in Norway from the accusation of being "German friendly." Instead Henrik Hauge represented Norway.

In fact, during his incarceration, Berggrav's attitude towards Germany had changed. He agreed with George Bell that it was wrong to employ saturation bombing against Dresden and with Bell also criticized the bombing of other German cities. But on the other hand, he was convinced that Germany must face a rigorous reckoning with her past. He was pleased to hear from Visser't Hooft that the Declaration had been freely given, but he noted that most of the signatories were those who had done much to oppose Hitler and suffered for it. In 1947, Berggrav maintained that the problem lay in the German mentality itself, which made possible National Socialism. This *German* attitude must be overcome by the Germans themselves. Such a way of thinking is consistent with his statement on the Treason Trials.

On the one hand, he approved of a just and humane dealing with Germany; on the other hand, he insisted upon a full accounting, not only by some convicted criminals against humanity, but by the German people as a whole. This attitude did not prevent him from being involved in a very strong defense of one German, who according to Berggrav, was never involved in any punishable offence during the war. Ernst Von Weizsäcker stood trial in Nurenberg in the summer of 1948 and Berggrav was called as a witness, together with Karl Barth and the former British Foreign Minister, Lord Halifax. Typical of Berggrav's character, he requested permission to shake hands with the accused Von Weizsäcker!

The accusing document with charges against Von Weizsäcker ran to 824 pages, but he was found guilty on only two charges. Meanwhile, Hans Schönfeld, a German on the staff of the World Council of Churches in Geneva, and Berggrav made an attempt to have him pardoned, which would have involved a personal visit to President Truman in May 1949. Illness prevented Berggrav from making that journey, but other initiatives were tried and eventually Von Weizsäcker was set free in October 1950.

Berggrav's view of the German mentality is substantiated by Dietrich Bonhoeffer in the document he wrote to his friends in 1943 shortly before being arrested. Bonhoeffer attempted to analyze what had happened in ten years of Nazi rule.

> Who would deny that in obedience, in their duty and calling, the Germans have again and again shown the utmost bravery and self-sacrifice? But the German has kept his freedom by seeking deliverance from personal decisions through serving within the community.
>
> Calling and freedom were two sides of the same coin. In this he misjudged the world; he did not realize that his submissiveness and self-sacrifice could be exploited for evil ends. When that happened, the exercise of the calling itself became questionable, and all the moral principles of the Germans were bound to totter. The fact could not be escaped that the German still lacked something fundamental; he could not see the need for free and responsible action, if needs be in opposition to his duty and his calling; in its place there appeared on the one hand, an irresponsible lack of scruple, and on the other, a self-tormenting punctiliousness that never led to action. Civil courage, in fact, can only grow out of the free responsibility of free men. Only now are the Germans beginning to discover the meaning of personal responsibility (*Letters and Papers from Prison* [SCM Press]).

If Berggrav could have read Bonhoeffer's views, he would likely have understood and agreed with the German pastor and theologian.

THE LUTHERAN WORLD FEDERATION

In the first flush of his enthusiasm for the Ecumenical Movement, Berggrav tended to criticize those who thought more of bringing the Lutheran churches of the world together than a World Council of Churches. However during the church struggle and the time given him to reflect in his cabin, he recognized more and more how important Luther was and how relevant his teachings were to the problems in the church. He attacked the German misuse of Luther, both in regard to anti-Semitism and their doctrine of the state. During the war, he criticized the Finnish Lutherans for receiving so warmly the German National Church representative of its Foreign Office, Bishop Theodor Haekel. Bishop Gulin of Helsinki complained of this and during a visit to Finland after the war, Berggrav was able to discuss the matter frankly with him and heal the rift. Berggrav gradually became convinced that a federation of Lutheran churches throughout the world would have an important role to play in the international responsibilities of the world church.

In November 1945, Berggrav visited the Archbishop of Canterbury in London. The occasion was to honor Berggrav with the decoration of the Lambeth Cross. While there, he was approached by a delegation of American Lutherans. Until that point he had refused to serve on a committee formed to explore the possibility of a Lutheran World Federation. The committee held both American and Swedish Lutherans and it had been thought that Berggrav refused to join the committee because of the passive attitude of Sweden during the war. They tried to persuade him to change his mind and join the committee. He promised that he would talk it over with his old friend, Erling Eidem, and subsequently they met in

Copenhagen a week before Christmas. Berggrav's real concern was that it looked as though the proposed Federation would be American dominated! He was also still concerned lest a strong Lutheran world organization, such as was proposed, would hinder the overall Ecumenical Movement. He thought that the Lutherans would have a stronger influence on the World Council of Churches if they sang in the choir with other Confessions than if they sang solo. His view was not held by the Americans or the Swedes, but they soon forgot their differences and invited Berggrav to be the speaker at the first Assembly of the Lutheran World Federation when it met in Lund in 1947. Originally, they planned to have the theme "The Lutheran Church and the State," but decided to leave that until the next Assembly in Hanover in 1952. Instead Berggrav and Otto Dibelius (Berlin) shared the theme of their experiences in the church struggle. At least one participant wrote later that it was the highpoint of the Assembly.

THE RESPONSIBILITY OF THE CHURCHES FOR INTERNATIONAL AFFAIRS

Before the war, Berggrav's main platform for ecumenical activity was the World Alliance, but as plans for the World Council of Churches developed, he saw that there was no room for both organizations. In a private letter to Henriod, the General Secretary of the Alliance, he drafted in broad outlines what he saw to be the future of the Alliance. He maintained that what the Alliance had taken as its mandate in 1914 could no longer be relevant. He proposed that instead of being a separate organization from the World Council of Churches, it should become a department of the World Council with well-defined objectives, which he described as being Christian planning for the international community "God's Word to the World." Berggrav saw the need for a department to monitor the world of politics, distribute factual information, and present alternative interpretations, the purpose being to give the churches an informed opinion on international affairs. These opinions could sometimes be expressed by individuals, sometimes by a group, sometimes by the World Council as a whole.

In this work, Berggrav saw two main issues. First, it is necessary that the church always proclaim God's Word. Sometimes this is done by an expression of principles or general comment upon an actual issue, such as the abuse of human rights in a country. But every such comment must contain a prophetic element, which goes beyond political reasoning and declares the Word of God. The judgment of the Word must be clear. Compromise and abstention are ruled out. The second issue Berggrav recognized was the need to identify who and what is addressed by the message of the church. It is the sinner who is addressed in every prophetic message, Berggrav said, and he applied the principle to actual political situations. His examples were the atom bomb, the treatment of refugees from the Soviet Union, and the Baltic question. In a conflict between two nations, the church of each nation must speak to its own people. The representatives of churches in the other countries can express their opinion, but that can never be the prophetic component of the message. Berggrav's main concern was the prophetic mandate of the church in international affairs and conflict between nations. He was insistent, however, that the prophetic voice could never be institutionalized. When the church speaks, it must do so with information about the facts and be ready to get involved.

Berggrav expressed his hope that a place would be found in the structure of the World Council for this important part of the church's responsibility in the world. Ultimately, the Commission of the Churches on International Affairs (CCIA) was established. Berggrav was proposed as the chairman of this commission by the Provisional Committee, but he had to resign because of ill health. He was unable to attend a meeting of the Commission in Cambridge, but he was appointed Deputy Chairman for the European Region.

After Berggrav's resignation, his deputy took over the chairmanship. He was no less than John Foster Dulles, who later became Secretary of State of the United States. He played a significant role in the preparations for the First Assembly in 1948 and was one of the principal speakers in Amsterdam.

THE FIRST ASSEMBLY OF THE WORLD COUNCIL OF CHURCHES

At 10:35 in the morning of August 23, 1948, the World Council of Churches was voted into being. That evening, Martin Niemöller, speaking at a public meeting in Amsterdam, said, "The 23rd of August, 1948, will be long remembered in the Christian world. Innumerable Christian people all over the world share our gratitude and joy, that a visible sign of our fraternal unity has at last been set up." The First Assembly followed with the overall theme of "Man's Disorder and God's Design." Quite early, Karl Barth made the comment that the theme should have been the other way round!

Berggrav spoke at a public meeting at the end of the Assembly, September 3, 1948. The date was ominous. On that day in 1939, the British heard that they were "in a state of war" with Germany. Nine years had passed and Berggrav spoke on "The Christian Witness in the International Disorder." The phrase that recurred through his speech was, "There is a foe." The audience knew that he had led the spiritual resistance to the foe in Norway and waited to hear something new. Berggrav called for

> the most exacting and most extensive of all human sacrifices: the sacrifice of instinctive emotions. It was felt necessary in wartime to whip up such emotions. Now our war practice is taking revenge. Primitive emotions for instance, as demonstrated and used by the world press, are today dominating mankind more than ever. A leading world paper wrote this year: "Let not our hatred of our foe grow cold." Without the sacrifice of some popular national emotions, those contrary to

God's law as well as to his love, destructive powers will gain ground and conquer man's best aspirations.

Then he repeated his theme phrase, *"There is a foe!"* The audience waited; Berggrav knew how to use his pauses in whatever language he spoke! He continued, "He is advancing today, gaining bridgeheads in all camps. He is very satisfied that no one points to him, but instead points to the West or the East. Indeed I know your question: Isn't it our duty sometimes to identify this foe with a person like Hitler or with a nation, or with an ideology." (Berggrav had listened to John Foster Dulles' attack on the evil of communism). He stated, "As a matter of fact, we did this during the Nazi-fight. Only I fear we did it too easily. We did it in the way that we were not only on the right side, but ourselves were through and through *all* right. Black and white were the colors and we were all white. Today, many are apt to judge in the same manner blacking either Communism or Capitalism."

He anticipated the reaction well: "What then? Something right and something wrong on both sides? No decisive judgement possible? No precise Christian witness?" But this was not his conclusion. They were rhetorical questions. Now came the thrust of his message:

> Surely there is a Christian witness. Where the means of the devil are used, there is the foe. Totalitarian police states are judged, not by their social structure, but by their satanic means. There can be no question as to the Christian witness so far. Not the churches, but God himself denounces the methods used by the totalitarian police states. Christians have to stick to the will of God and the rights endowed upon man by him—not by nature. Here the Christian witness means resistance unto the last drop of blood.

This statement attacked the draft of the United Nations' Declaration of Human Rights. The American Declaration of Independence of 1776, upon which the Preamble of the United Nations' Declaration was based, describes the rights of man as endowed upon him by "his Creator." The United Nations had dropped the term "Creator" and replaced it with the word "nature." The alternation seemed to many to be innocuous, but not to Berggrav. He saw the change as a deliberate attempt to deny the sovereignty of God: "There is a living God, and we must proclaim his will. It is never utopian to proclaim the will of God," he said. This very significant speech was based upon four propositions:

> There is a living God.
> God is law and love, order and sacrifice.
> There is a foe.
> There is a victory.

Memories of the war so recently ended helped him to draw upon the courage of so many present at that meeting. Looking at the devastated Europe in 1948, he could say that while victory may seem remote,

> how remote was victory in 1940? Nobody knew. But then we all said: however far it may be never let it out of sight, always think of it, always look for it. Solidarity was felt as already anticipating victory. How much more is this the case now, if we bow under God's solidarity with men and direct all our enthusiasm to the achievement of a future.

He called upon the churches to accept their responsibility of appealing to the nations so that they recognize the overriding authority of the eternal laws of the Creator. Such was the nature of Berggrav's involvement in the Ecumenical Movement. He believed that if the combined voice of the churches spoke, the United Nations would listen. So he had thought throughout the time of his house arrest, when he sent a letter illegally to the Catholic Archbishop Preysing in Berlin suggesting that the Pope and the World Council of Churches should act together or at least in parallel to halt the atrocities being committed throughout Europe.

One is reminded of Bonhoeffer, who in 1934 appealed to the Ecumenical Council, in solidarity, to halt the drift to war. Bonhoeffer's words to the World Alliance then were:

> Only the one great ecumenical council of the holy church of Christ over all the world can speak so that the world, though it gnash its teeth, will have to hear, so that the people will rejoice because the church of Christ in the name of Christ has taken the weapons from the hands of its sons, forbidden war, and proclaimed the peace of Christ against the raging world.

Bonhoeffer was only 28, but the much older Berggrav, in more sober mood, held precisely the same faith. Both men knew, in different situations that the church must speak as one if the world was to hear the Word of God. Berggrav made this call to the Roman Catholic Archbishop and then after the war he made the same appeal to the Scandinavian church leaders.

Berggrav's speech in Amsterdam was much discussed; he pressed for action to have the phrase "laws of the Creator" restored instead of leaving "by nature" in its place. In February 1949 at a meeting of the Central Committee of the WCC, at the Ecumenical Center in the Chateau de Bossey, Switzerland, Berggrav urged action on this issue. He was disappointed at the response. Some members thought he was being naïve, but George Bell and Martin Niemöller supported him. He was asked to put his ideas into a document, which could be considered by the CCIA. By the middle of April, Visser't Hooft received a nine-page document, copies of which Berggrav had sent to Arnold Toynbee, John Foster Dulles, Max Huber, Erik Wolf and Josef Hromadka. Visser't Hooft was skeptical of the proposal and wrote to Berggrav that the relation between "natural law" and "laws of the Creator" was a complicated theological issue. He reminded Berggrav that ecumenical theology was christologically centered in matters of ethics and not in "natural law" or "creation theology." Nonetheless, the Central Committee of the WCC, meeting in the summer of 1949, found many members positive about Berggrav's initiative and decided upon a conference to deal with Christian views on International Law.

Berggrav's initial proposal to draft an alternative preamble for the Document on Human Rights was not realized. On the other hand his involvement in the general work of CCIA and questions of international affairs occupied him over the next few years. He also attempted, through many articles and lectures, to strengthen the strategy of the WCC in this area.

ECUMENICAL ACTIVITY AND THE COLD WAR

In his document written in April 1949, which led to the conference on International Law, Berggrav had also sketched out principles for the involvement of the WCC in actual conflicts, of which he listed five examples:

> The tension between the Soviet Union and the West
>   (the Cold War)
> The violation of human rights
> The question of Germany
> Racial discrimination
> The Palestinian questions

Of these five problem areas, Berggrav concentrated at first on the role that the WCC should play in the cold war and in particular on relations with the churches behind the Iron Curtain. At first, Berggrav was very skeptical of the theory that the balance of equal powers (the United States and the Union of Soviet Socialist Republics) was a means of preserving peace. He had frequently spoken against the use of the atomic bomb. On August 12, 1945, six days after the bombing of Hiroshima, Berggrav addressed a congregation of the Allied Forces in Norway, taking his theme "The Devil's Weapon." Satan is a "master of destruction," he asserted, "look at his new angel in disguise during this past week." A note on the manuscript of the sermon leaves no doubt that what he meant was the bombing of Hiroshima. He went on to say, "The principle of life is constructive and consists of gathering together and building up. But now, the atomic bomb and with it unknown powers of destruction, beyond anything we have known before, are made possible." He warned that under the cloak of science there could be a hidden devil we cannot see.

When the Executive Committee of the WCC met in Toronto in February 1950, it spoke out against the hydrogen bomb, which it described as "the latest and most terrible step in the crescendo of warfare which has changed war from a fight between men and nations to a mass murder of human life." Then it added: "All men have responsibilities before God as they face the grave issues raised by the hydrogen bomb and other weapons of modern war.... The governments of the nations have an inescapable responsibility at this hour. The world is divided into hostile camps through suspicion and distrust and through the failure of the nations to bring their mutual relations within an agreed system of justice and order. As representatives of Christian churches we appeal for a gigantic new effort for peace."

The urgency of this statement was due to President Truman's instruction to the United States Atomic Energy Committee on January 31, 1950 to continue work on all atomic weapons, including the hydrogen bomb. The Executive Committee statement was generally approved by Berggrav although he had certain reservations about its details.

THE CHURCHES OF EASTERN EUROPE

Since its formation in Amsterdam, the WCC was divided politically. The controversy between John Foster Dulles and Josef Hromadka continued and attracted supporters for one side or another. Berggrav saw the danger of the WCC becoming too politically involved. He insisted that the Ecumenical Movement united churches of all lands regardless of their political allegiances. The WCC should cross all political frontiers. This led him to be concerned more and more about the membership of churches in Eastern Europe. Unlike Niemöller, whose line was one of reconciliation between East and West,

Berggrav insisted that the division was not to do with political systems but with freedom. As early as his report on Amsterdam in 1948, he maintained that the role of the church is not to enter into political discussions or to take sides in conflicting political systems. As the years passed, he became more and more worried by the political involvement of the WCC.

Despite this clear statement, or perhaps because of it, he came into conflict with Visser't Hooft about the membership of the Russian Orthodox Church. He warned the General Secretary that the Russian Orthodox delegation would make political capital out of his invitation to them to visit Geneva and discuss membership of the WCC. Visser't Hooft took his comments seriously, answering, "Your warnings are understood. At the same time, I believe that we must continue our negotiations with the Russians on the basis of principles, which were laid down for our ecumenical work." However, Visser't Hooft recognized the dangerous factors in the situation.

Berggrav could never quite forget that in Amsterdam he had raised the case of the Hungarian Bishop who spoke out critically against the communist government and was imprisoned for his openness. He called for some action, but got little support. About that incident, he later wrote, "Sadly, I had the impression that we should have called the Council 'The World Council of Caution.' " He deplored the lack of will to call such interference in the life of the church by its proper name. He started a campaign on behalf of Bishop Ordass and wrote a strong letter of protest to the Prime Minister of Hungary. His letter was translated and published in the Hungarian newspaper—with commentary. Bishop Ordass was in prison, the commentary read, not for political reasons, but because of certain financial irregularities. In the years that followed, tensions grew between Berggrav and the WCC on the attitude towards the churches in the East of Europe.

In 1956, Berggrav gave an interview to a Danish paper about a delegation of Danish church leaders who were invited to visit the Soviet Union. His intervention displeased Visser't

Hooft who wrote that "this last outburst on the part of Berggrav is liable to disrupt delicate discussions going on between the WCC and the Moscow Patriarchate."

THE GREEK CHILDREN

Berggrav continued as a member of the Executive Committee, in spite of differences with the General Secretary. He supported the WCC on many issues and in turn was supported by the WCC. One of these was the question of the Greek children separated from their parents during the war. In 1950, the problem was described in a report by the International Red Cross. This report was followed by a telegram from Archbishop Spyridon of Athens to the WCC. Many thousands of Greek children were being held in Eastern European lands. On January 12, 1950, Berggrav and Arnulf Øverland, a well-known radical author, signed a protest with the title "Abduction of Children." In it, they asserted that "For us, the rights of parents are fundamental."

This action was not popular in Norway; some in Geneva also expressed serious reservations. Fears of the Cold War becoming "warm" were growing. A third world war between two superpowers, each with nuclear capability, seemed too horrendous to contemplate. Berggrav took the initiative and persuaded the Executive Committee of the WCC to write to Archbishop Spyridon. He even drafted the letter. In it he put forward the Christian conviction that the children should be returned to their parents, a conviction firmly based upon the right of the parents.

Berggrav's attitude toward Eastern Europe needs to be understood. He would have nothing to do with anti-Communist propaganda, such as plagued America under McCarthy. He could see that some nations might choose to have a communist system, others a capitalist. The church had no part in deciding which was right for that particular nation, certainly not from outside, but he was opposed to the totalitarian practices of the communist states and the inhuman methods used in those regimes. When the Second Assembly of the WCC was to be held in the United States, the McCarthy dominated regime refused visas to delegates from communist countries. Berggrav protested and when Josef Hromadka from Czechoslovakia was not to be allowed to come, he raised his voice powerfully.

This was not the first time Berggrav had criticized the United States. After a speech by President Truman on September 28, 1951, Berggrav wrote a letter to the WCC in which he pointed out the danger of equating the things of God with the things of the Western powers. He also pointed out that the churches in the West were becoming dangerously near to being used as instruments of western politics.

When in 1953 *Time* magazine brought out a summary of Berggrav's "attack" on the church life of America, it quoted him as saying, "The American churches often appear to have two altars, one for God and another for the Dollar!" In the following year during a long visit to the United States (including the Second Assembly of the WCC in Evanston), Berggrav was asked in an interview what most impressed him about the nation. To a rather surprised interviewer, he said, "the quarter." Berggrav quickly added, "Because on it is inscribed, 'In God we trust.' " The reporter was confused; Berggrav explained, "It is *not* true."

Berggrav was neither anti-American nor anti-Russian, but criticized both. He retained to the end the ability to see both sides of an argument without committing himself to either. He never strove to be popular or in any way "play to the gallery," keeping a fiercely independent mind.

LAST ASSEMBLY

Although it was only the Second Assembly of the WCC, it was Berggrav's last. He had already become more involved with the work of the Bible Societies. But at Evanston in 1954, he was prominent and much loved. Canon Herklots, a British delegate and the author of the popular report on Evanston, gives us a glimpse of Berggrav in action. When the Assembly met first for worship, Berggrav, as one of the six presidents of the WCC, led the congregation in reciting the Apostles' Creed. He led it first in German and then asked each to say it in his or her own tongue.

In one of the later sessions, Berggrav was chairing a meeting at which Otto Dibelius of Berlin was to speak. Herklots describes the scene.

> When we arrived, just a little late, Bishop Berggrav of Norway, the leader of Christian resistance to totalitarian oppression in Norway during the time of war, was speaking from the chair. He had already endeared himself to the Assembly by his humor and directness. He had spoken of the healing power of love between individuals and the need for healing love between churches. Then he said, "Any church prestige is doomed by Christ himself. There exists *no master church* above the others. What we have got is a church family in Christ. Unity in Christ has started changing the world church atmosphere. The tensions of evil have been forced to be on the defensive. This does not mean that we should make a sweet soup of the mess we are in. Jesus himself never did make such a soup of the world affairs. He spoke out directly about any injustice and violation. He took a firm stand against lies and falsifications, against God-denying wickedness of all sorts. He was in solidarity with sinful men, but not in solidarity with sin. He was the Prince of Peace, but never a prince of war disguised in a mantle of peace." Then he introduced Bishop Dibelius, who began by telling of the Confessing Church in Germany during the Nazi Regime, quoting the Barmen Declaration of 1934, the sheet anchor of the church resistance. It was a story Berggrav knew well. His own experiences during the Nazi Occupation had followed a similar course. When Dibelius ended, he simply said, "The acoustics in this hall are bad. This afternoon they have been good. You

have *heard* what we mean" (H.G.G. Herklots, *Looking at Evanston* [SCM Press, 1954]).

Two other speakers followed Dibelius that hot Sunday afternoon: Reinhold Niebuhr and Josef Hromadka who, thanks to Berggrav's strong protest, was granted a visa to visit Evanston.

THE ECUMENICAL MOVEMENT IN NORWAY

The impression given at large world gatherings of the churches under the auspices of the WCC was often that church leaders were ready to cooperate with one another but found it difficult to put this spirit of cooperation into practice when they went home. In the years after the war, Berggrav traveled so much abroad to these conferences that he might well have neglected the task of union at home. But from the moment of the entry of the Norwegian church into the WCC, he played a central role at home.

For many years, Berggrav was the driving force of the Ecumenical Movement in Norway. By 1951, participation was institutionalized with the formation of the Norwegian Institute for Inter-Church Relations. Earlier, he and Visser't Hooft had been responsible for organizing a World Congress for Christian Youth in Oslo. The Congress was opened on July 22, 1947, in a hall of a Pentecostal church. Hundreds of youth came from 70 countries. Berggrav made quite an impression on the young people and the Congress itself did much to improve the ecumenical climate in Norway. Contacts between the dominant Lutheran Church of Norway and the Free Churches were strengthened. Surely, Berggrav had this experience in mind in Evanston when he said, "There exists no master church above the others. What we have got is a church family in Christ."

In the autumn of 1950, Berggrav gave a lecture on the theme of "Christian Fellowship at Home and Abroad." In this lecture he tried to uncover the reasons why ecumenical work had been so weak in Norway. He suggested that what was needed was a forum or exploratory group to look into the matter.

An immediately favorable reaction to this suggestion helped to establish a "Contact Group." On December 19, 1950, a few days before he gave up his episcopal office, he was invited to its first meeting. One of the participants, a Baptist, characterized the meeting as a successful ecumenical forum "with Berggrav as the inspiration and most jovial center of it all."

In the years following World War II, Eivind Berggrav was, without doubt, at the very center of the Ecumenical Movement. His interests in the movement were rooted in his experience of two devastating world wars and his pastoral desire to see the church flourish in its faith and ministry. Berggrav could not, of course, have foreseen where the Ecumenical Movement or the World Council of Churches would lead the church by the end of the 20th century. Yet his passion to make the church's faith a faith in Christ who is "Lord of all" (Acts 10:36), meaningful and vital on the world scene, drove him to explore all opportunities to build bridges. From 1946 until his death in 1959, his greatest concern was for the health and growth of the United Bible Societies and the task of bringing God's Word to people.

12

The Church's Common Task

As Protestant missions expanded throughout the world at the end of the 18th century, missionaries became aware of the weaknesses caused by their division into different denominations. Those differences had often resulted from deeply held convictions, almost always based upon a reading of the Bible! But against the questions and concepts of non-Christian religions, the theological disputes of Europe appeared somewhat parochial, perhaps irrelevant. William Carey, the pioneer Baptist missionary and a distinguished translator of the Bible into many languages, called for a world conference to be held in South Africa in 1810. His call had to wait a hundred years, but in 1910 a World Missionary Conference was convened in Edinburgh. Its purpose was officially defined as "research and conference regarding missionary work and problems" when faced with non-Christian religions. No resolutions regarding doctrine or church policy were to be entertained on which the churches or societies might take different views. The World Student Christian Federation also played a significant role.

Although Berggrav was teaching at Eidsvoll and lecturing throughout Scandinavia at this time, he must have been aware of the implications of this large conference in Edinburgh, where 1200 delegates represented the Missionary Societies of the principal Protestant churches of the world. That conference gave rise to the International Missionary Council. For all their differences, one treasure these missionary societies had in common was the Bible. In fact, they were already being serviced by an ecumenical organization, which had been started a century before: the Bible Society Movement. Every missionary society at Edinburgh had depended upon one or other of the Bible Societies. The American Bible Society went further than any other ecumenical organization by inviting the Roman Catholics to join them. The acceptance of that invitation had to wait.

Plans for cooperation between both churches and Bible Societies made some progress in the years following World War I and the pace quickened in the 1930s. By 1939, plans for what was later to become the World Council of Churches were in place, as well as for further cooperation between the American and the British Bible Societies. The war shattered most plans. The progress towards the formation of the World Council of Churches as well as towards the United Bible Societies (UBS) was rapid after World War II and they had close parallels. The UBS was officially brought into being on July 11, 1946, the WCC on August 23, 1948. Berggrav was involved at the highest level in both and both had a long period of waiting.

THE FORMATION OF THE UNITED BIBLE SOCIETIES

The first modern Bible Society, with its worldwide—ecumenical—missionary outlook and commitment to serving the churches as an independent agency, was the British and Foreign Bible Society formed in 1804. Its stated aim was "to encourage the wider circulation of the Holy Scriptures without note or comment." From the beginning it was intended to serve not only the churches of Britain but also countries in Europe and the British colonies. Within a few years, the American Bible Society was founded in 1816, again serving more than the American churches, but also helping American missionaries by providing Bibles in the languages of the people they sought to evangelize. By the end of the 19th century the British and Foreign Bible Society and the American Bible Society had spanned the world with a network of agencies and associations.

The Netherlands Bible Society (founded 1814) and the National Bible Society of Scotland (founded in 1861 from two existing Bible Societies in Glasgow and Edinburgh) both served other countries than their own, with which they had special links. All the other national Bible Societies served only their own country providing Bibles for their churches. Norway, for example, provided only Norwegian Bibles until Berggrav, once the UBS was formed, took over responsibility also for Madagascar.

When World War II came to an end, Europe lay in ruins, offering unlimited work for the Bible Societies. The idea of a Council of Bible Societies had grown before and during the war, but it was a bold step on behalf of the two major Bible Societies to call the first non-governmental conference in bomb-scarred Britain as early as May 1946. The host was George Bell, then Bishop of Chichester, in whose diocesan conference center Elfinsward the historic international meeting occurred. The decision to form the United Bible Societies as soon as "six of the Bible Societies, eligible for membership officially approved the charter." By July 11, 1946, the sixth letter of approval arrived.

BERGGRAV AND JOHN TEMPLE

On Tuesday, September, 18, 1945, Berggrav was visited by one of the General Secretaries of the British and Foreign Bible Society, the Reverend John Temple, a Methodist who had served as a missionary in China. He had come to invite Berggrav to speak at a conference of Bible Societies in England. He explained that apart from the four initiating Bible Societies of America, Britain, the Netherlands and Scotland, several European Bible Societies were being considered for an invitation to attend. He expressed the hope that Norway would be represented and Berggrav would be one of the main speakers. Berggrav was impressed by his visitor, but before he answered, he went over to the corner of the room and pulled out a bag of books. He had prepared the bag in anticipation of his arrest in the dark days of 1942; he wanted to have with him a Bible, a Greek New Testament and a Concordance to help him with translation work. Berggrav spoke of his experiences and of the way in which the Bible had been his guide in very difficult situations during the war. Temple soon had the impression that he had found a significant church leader who would help the world in future Bible work. Later, he spoke of these conversations as one of the greatest privileges of his life. His colleagues in London also noted how his eyes lit up when he spoke about this visit. Berggrav, soon to be deeply involved in the work of the United Bible Societies, later remarked, "Temple sun-shined me into the movement!" Berggrav had a way of inventing words in English. Temple had obviously stimulated him—like a ray of sunshine in dark days.

In the following year (1946), Berggrav had many invitations to visit England and to speak about his experiences during the occupation of Norway. Among his most important engagements was the Bible conference at Elfinsward, May 6–9. He was not only there as a speaker, but as chairman of the Conference. In addition to the four initiating societies, representatives were present from Czechoslovakia, Denmark, Finland, France, Germany, Poland, Sweden, Switzerland, and Norway.

Only a few months before, Berggrav had spoken in the Cathedral of St. Pierre in Geneva at that February meeting.

> I was wondering how it would be again to meet Christians from all over the world. My surprise is that it is no surprise at all. It seems so obvious, because in these years we have lived closer to one another than in times when we could more easily communicate. We prayed more together, we listened more together to the

Word of God, our hearts were more together. During the war, Christ has told us: "My Christians, you are one."

Those simple words vibrated through the sessions of the Provisional Committee preparing for the formation of the World Council of Churches and raised the discussion above the level of strategy and organization. Now at Elfinsward, Eivind Berggrav would be chairing another preparatory meeting for the formation of a world council of Bible Societies.

ELFINSWARD

A young American Baptist, who later became a world-renowned expert on translation (and not only Bible translation) was present at this conference of Bible Societies in England. He was Eugene Nida and his report captures the atmosphere perfectly:

> In the early May 1946, the weather was typically cold and rainy, but inside the meeting room there was the warm glow of renewed friendship by old friends who had not seen each other during the long dark years of World War II. We had all come through London and had seen the sprawling wasteland of rubble in the center of the city and realized it must be far worse in Rotterdam, Dresden and Stalingrad. In London, St. Paul's Cathedral and the nearby Bible House were standing like symbols of hope.

Further on in the report, Nida judged the mood of the conference:

> We were all profoundly influenced by the sense of overwhelming urgency to meet the spiritual need of the churches in eastern Europe, the countless refugees in Asia, and the rapidly growing number of believers in Sub-Saharan Africa. Colonialism was becoming a thing of the past, and the rise of two superpowers raised the threat of total atomic destruction. Under such circumstances it was not easy to make plans, but it was also no

time to be concerned about traditional ways of doing things. Old rivalries had to be forgotten.

He quickly added, "Elfinsward profoundly changed the Bible Society movement and radically changed my life."

After the sharing of experiences from Poland and Germany, from Britain and America, which gave a rounded picture of the witness of the world church and the network of Bible Societies, Berggrav in typical fashion turned the eyes of all to the present situation and to the future. The third session of the conference, chaired by Berggrav, took the theme "The Remaking of Europe."

The solidarity of the Christian community across the cracks of war was a matter of deep concern to Berggrav. As early as World War I he had felt the horror of Christians fighting against Christians. In an earlier session, he had made that dramatic gesture of welcoming Hanns Lilje with an embrace, leaving the platform to do so. More than a renewal of contact with an old friend; this was a symbol demonstrating the struggle of the *church* against National Socialism. In this personal contact he expressed the unity of the Christian community across all frontiers. His first speech on the remaking of Europe emphasized the need of remaking at the personal or individual level. Speaking to this theme, he urged a practical approach; rhetoric would not be enough. He challenged those present with the assertion that the conference should follow the realistic and not the romantic line. "After all," he said, "the Bible is realistic, not optimistic."

In the short speech with which he opened that third session, Berggrav made clear his own attitude to the Bible and its use in evangelism:

> When we are confronted with the Bible we have to face big things which are significant in the remaking of Europe. We might well have put "the world" and not just "Europe," for I think it is the same situation all over the world as to the Bible. The world needs remaking, and at once when you mention the world, you

think of the politics of today and the future that is possible for mankind. I think we ought first to think of us here and of all mankind as individuals and of remaking the individual. Every one of us is in need of being remade. What is the significance of the Bible in that? In wartime and especially in occupation time, the Bible explained itself to us. It is the usual experience all over the world that when a man is in need of God's Word, he gets it in the Bible, but when he is in no need, he finds the Bible a very difficult book to read.

Berggrav spoke from personal experience, not only in the dark days of war, but recalling his own early struggles with the Bible. This was not the time to say it, but he could have told of a young man going home in the night train wrestling with his Bible and determining *to do away with it*. He wanted to be a free thinker, not hemmed in by Christian doctrine. He had even resolved to burn his confirmation Bible. Symbolically he did. Freedom enticed him and the Bible stood in his way. But he came through that agony of a lost faith and for the rest of his life he valued the Bible as the prime witness to God's love in Christ and as the source of his faith and life.

At the end of this session, he was honest and direct. The Bible does not have all the answers. He concluded:

We have all voiced our unity in the Bible which means so much to the world today. When people are looking for a united church today there is only one Bible and that adds very much to the significance of the Bible in remaking the world and Europe. But, the Bible has no ready-made solutions and remedies for everything. You need to find them out for yourself by the guidance of the Spirit.

A World Task

After Elfinsward and the decision of the first six Bible Societies to join together, many other Societies expressed interest in the United Bible Society. A committee agreed to hear reports of need from all these Societies at a further meeting in

Amersfoort the following year (1947). It took a whole day to hear the reports of post-war needs in many lands—a famine for the Word of God. Berggrav was deeply moved and responded with a clear vision of the future for the United Bible Societies, to which he would always add "of the world":

> All these figures we have been given are spiritual figures, they are from God. I would say that this day is the day of baptism of the UBS. It is the first time that we have had the global view and we have met with Christ.... We are now in the happy and blessed situation that we are called upon to be His agents in answering this call.

The Executive Committee of the UBS, under the chairmanship of Berggrav, began work setting up the structure to answer that call. John Temple had already been invited to become General Secretary and this was confirmed. Berggrav was disappointed that the British and Foreign Bible Society released him only for part-time work. He was expected to remain in his London office, although he was relieved of some administration duties "that he might give the greater part of his time to the new assignment." Berggrav recognized a certain lack of enthusiasm with the BFBS. When John Temple died in China, November 30, 1948, Berggrav expressed his concern:

> My only real concern would be if the BFBS *Committee* should be regretting that it invited us to start the UBS and put in the "machinery." To my mind we have not at all too much machinery. A full-time General Secretary seems to me to be a condition which, if not realized, would show that we did not take ourselves or the UBS seriously. On the other hand, I can quite well see that machinery as such is dangerous in the antechamber of the Kingdom of God, but we never had too much of it. A half-time General Secretary would not be master of his time and would always have to ask permission from his real master.

That letter to William Platt of the BFBS helped him to convince the Committee that a full-time General Secretary was necessary for the work of the UBS. John Temple was succeeded by Olivier Béguin, whose wartime and post-war work with prisoners of war had given him experience of Bible distribution and pastoral ministry. He was already in Geneva working as an Assistant Secretary and was required to move to London. Berggrav had expressed his preference for the UBS to be centered in London, but he also wanted a link with the WCC in Geneva. He got both in Béguin.

In the early days of the United Bible Societies, Berggrav was able to bring a new element into the Bible Society world. For a long time London and New York had dominated the scene and Berggrav brought in the voice of the smaller societies, helping to make them also part of an international enterprise. It was not easy. Berggrav used to joke about his naïvity. What did he know of the complexities of international Bible work? Yet his leadership eased the tendency of the two giant societies to polarize. He encouraged and enabled both to make sacrifices of their proud inheritance so that there might be a single organization called the United Bible Societies of the world, with even the small societies and agencies of Europe as part of the world scene.

A TRIBUTE

On the centenary of Berggrav's birth in 1984, the UBS published a booklet to commemorate the occasion. It contains a series of articles on the Bishop as a Bible Society man. Boyd L. Daniels has a brief evaluation of the man:

> In the critical early years of the new fellowship, he played a singularly important role. One can assess that role only by looking closely at the man himself: for his contribution was not so much in providing intellectual formulations or organizational structures as in being a person of vision who had a sincere love of the Bible and a pastor's desire to share its good news with others. Those who knew him speak of his warmth, his open-mindedness, his realism, and his sense of humor, his

humility. They note his ecumenical instincts, his missionary zeal. Above all they comment on his inner strength, his deep and abiding faith in God and in Jesus Christ as revealed in the Bible. All these things together and the plus factor which made the man more than just the sum of these parts became the stuff of which extraordinary leadership was compounded; and the emerging UBS was the beneficiary. (UBS Papers, Global Office, Reading, U.K.)

CHAIRMAN AND FIRST PRESIDENT

While John Temple was still General Secretary, before Berggrav was appointed the first President of the UBS, he chaired three vital meetings of the infant organization: Elfinsward in 1946, the first UBS Executive Committee in Amersfoort in June 1947, and its first Council meeting in Dunblane in Scotland in June 1948, which was John Temple's last.

An immediate affinity developed between Berggrav and the new General Secretary, Olivier Béguin, who had been at Elfinsward representing the WCC. When Temple was General Secretary in London Béguin held the fort in Geneva as Assistant. One conviction Berggrav and Béguin shared was the need to involve the European Bible Societies in work outside their own country. Berggrav himself set an example, commenting he said:

> One of the representatives of the big societies said that the kind of Bible Society that was engaged in only providing books for its own national area was a selfish Bible Society. It was merely trading in the Word of God; it printed and sold Bibles, and used the profit to provide its own people with more books. It had no heart for all the millions in the colonial world and elsewhere who had no Bibles at all.

> My first impression on listening to these words, he said was that the man had spoken neither law nor justice. We had done our duty, and that was a fact! But his

harsh words proved to be a call from God. (UBS Papers, Global Office, Reading, U.K.)

Once Berggrav recognized these words as a call from God, he was not slow to take action. He returned to Norway and met his board, telling them "that we were egoistic and full of business motives and that we lacked vision and the real purpose of a Bible Society." The Board was shaken by these words as Berggrav had been. Not all reacted as he did. Some complained that they had a constitution to which they were required to adhere. This did not allow for work outside Norway except the Norwegians serving abroad. "Then" said Berggrav, "we must change the constitution." Norway had a special relationship with Madagascar and Berggrav expressed his concern that they should not leave the cost of distributing Bibles there to the British Society. Before long the constitution was changed and the Norwegian Bible Society bore the cost of Bibles produced in London for Madagascar. Not only was it necessary to change the constitution but new methods of fundraising also had to be devised. Yet, within a few years, the Norwegian Bible Society was not only providing the finances, a Norwegian printing firm had taken on the responsibility of producing the Malagasy Bible. Other bold steps followed, among them support for the Boros Bible and securing finances for translating the Bible into Mbum. At the same time the work in Norway grew faster than ever before.

As chairman and later as president of the UBS, Berggrav was able to share the Norwegian experience with several of the other small societies of Europe. Steadily the influence grew and several of these Societies became actively involved in the overseas work of the UBS.

The first meeting of the UBS Council after the death of John Temple was held in New York during June 1949. Berggrav was not there. His multifarious activities with much travel and endless committees of the WCC and UBS, together with repeated demands to lecture, preach, and conduct seminars, had their effect. Berggrav was ill and realized that he must cut down on his activities. He sent a message to the UBS Council, explaining why he could not attend and that he wished to resign from the Standing Committee and also as UBS Chairman. A cable was sent to Bishop Berggrav from the Council meeting:

> Council United Bible Societies sends most loving greetings. It pledges effective cooperation for great cause. We are ever grateful your inspiring leadership. They who wait on the Lord shall renew their strength.

Characteristic of Berggrav, in his message to the Council he asked to remain the representative of the Norwegian Bible Society. On consideration of their loss of a chairman, the UBS appointed Bishop Berggrav its first President and he served them as such for eight years. He was less involved now in chairing the business sessions or the detailed work of the Standing Committee, but he remained an inspiring leader while Olivier Béguin further organized the UBS and expanded its work. Dr. Eric North of the American Bible Society took over as Chairman.

PRESIDENT AS PREACHER

The United Bible Societies leadership heard some challenging—and at times disquieting—sermons during those eight years of Berggrav's presidency.

The 1950 conference of the UBS Standing Committee was held at Matlock in England and the President was invited to give the introductory meditation. He took "Earthen Vessels" as his theme, relying upon the words of St. Paul in 2 Corinthians 4:6–7: "For God who commanded the light to shine out of darkness, hath shined in our hearts, to give the light of the knowledge of the glory of God in the face of Jesus Christ. But we have this treasure in earthen vessels, that the excellency of the power may be of God and not of us." The text came alive in his hands, fresh and unexpected. He began comfortably:

> When in my early years as pastor, I read these verses, I was consoled by the phrase "earthen vessels." I had

very soon to confess to myself that I was not the adequate man for God's message. All of you may have had a feeling like this from time to time, or often or always—the feeling that you are quite inadequate to fulfil the idea of a servant of the Gospel. And then it was a consolation to have the confirmation of Holy Scripture that we are but "earthen vessels."

After a dramatic pause, Berggrav opened up his heart to his fellow Christians: "But I was wrong! That was not at all the point." He went on to say that, while the text was heartening, it was not consoling. It did not make us satisfied with our work. "The real point is that there is a light shining in the darkness, shining in our hearts, which must be seen by other men." Berggrav never preached at his congregation; he preached with them. At this point he began to share his own sense of failure: "I feel condemned by this word, for I know that what is said is not true of me. You can never examine yourself and find out whether you are shining, for surely your self-examination will always tell you that you are not." In one of those familiar images of self disapproval, he said "I am more of a cloud than I am a sunbeam."

In applying the text to the work at hand, Berggrav noted,

Bible Societies and Bible Society men are quite earthen, as are our troubles and our problems. There are no sunbeams in our program for the day, it just consists of matter. But I tell you that God is shining in this matter. The Bible is his concentrated sunlight. The book itself consists of "earthen" paper and black print, but its transcendent power is not created by our production of Bibles. However, if we stopped producing the "earthen vessels," God would lose his tool and his mirror for men. Our daily work is done in darkness, but the glory of God in the face of Jesus Christ actually uses our difficulties with the matter and the methods and the "earthen" arrangements in order to get the opportunities for becoming available as the transcendent light in the world.

With the clarity that marked all his sermons and devotional comments, he summarized, "And so we are not *consoled*, but rather encouraged and made responsible for the earthen vessels and not for the heavenly power. He gives that to us, in spite of our darkness. Step into the sunshine; the darkness is gone."

The Bible Societies were to hear many such addresses in the next seven years. Outstanding among them were those in Vienna, 1950, at the centenary of Bible Society work in Austria; the 150th anniversary of the BFBS in 1954 in London; and on numerous occasions of celebration and also at routine meetings of the UBS. Berggrav often drew upon his experiences during the war, and he always combined challenge, even criticism, with encouragement and hope.

BERGGRAV AND PAUL'S LETTER TO THE PHILIPPIANS

During his internment, Berggrav undertook two writing tasks: his childhood memories and a new translation of the Letter to the Philippians. The circumstances of imprisonment gave him a sense of kinship with the Apostle Paul; it was no accident that he concentrated his mind on the "Prison Letters." The choice of Philippians was not surprising, because as early as 1925 he had chosen this text as his theme for the obligatory lecture prior to his disputation. The third chapter in particular echoed his lifelong urge to stretch out beyond the boundaries. He saw in this chapter a confirmation of his own belief that the Christian way of life was not a static model, but was constantly pushing at the limits, growing and changing with new insights and new experiences.

After the war, Berggrav published a new translation of Philippians with the title *An Experiment with the Letter to the Philippians*. Berggrav had found the Letter meaningful to him during his internment and wished to convey that meaning in the translation. Already in the thirties, he had seen the importance of translating the Bible into a relevant and lively language so that the next generation would understand could understand God's Word. At first, he began to work on the biblical history. When he became Bishop of Oslo and President of the Norwegian Bible Society, he lost no time in proposing a new Norwegian translation of the New Testament. In May 1939, he had the agreement of the Board to undertake an experiment, attempting to translate the Bible into modern speech.

Obviously, Berggrav's teaching experience, his episcopal visits, and his work among children all led him to see the need for a modern translation. The existing translation, although loved by the older people, was far removed from the language of the young, to whom it seemed remote and irrelevant in the modern world. There was, of course, opposition from those who found any new translation inappropriate, because it did not "sound right" or because it was not as easy to commit to memory. But Berggrav argued that the Bible might be dropped from the schools if students did not use a more intelligible translation. A New Testament for young people was proposed. Berggrav remained a member of the committee and he examined every draft and worked on the translation himself during a regular weekly meeting with a distinguished New Testament scholar. This work on the Youth Translation later appeared in 1978 and 1985. A distinguish professor who had taken a leading part in these later translations commented that Berggrav was the man "who had vision for a new translation and put into motion the initiative for its realization. He not only had the basic idea, but was a kind of 'locomotive' which sent the project on its way."

Ten Years Old

In celebration of the tenth anniversary of the founding of the UBS in 1946, Béguin asked Berggrav to write a commemorative article for the *UBS Bulletin* that would be a presidential or "State of the Union" address. Such an article was not his style, but Berggrav indicated that he would give a "fireside chat." Reviewing the past, he outlined the successes and failures of the UBS, but typically concentrated upon the greatness of the task ahead. "A ten-year-old has no reason for great festivities," he began, "for these are only justified when one has the feeling of having accomplished something, or at least of having some sense of satisfaction with one's achievements. Yet the UBS feels anything but satisfied. After ten years of existence we do not look to past achievements, but forward knowing that very big tasks lie ahead." Berggrav recognized the enormous task that God had laid upon this ministry—far beyond limited human powers. He added, "Whenever God wishes to bless a man or a fellowship he makes overwhelming demands upon them, so that they shall realize how inadequate they themselves are." With this introduction he outlined the way forward. He did not hesitate to criticize what had been done, nor to underestimate the immensity of the task ahead, but it was a clarion call to rely on God's grace and strength.

Visser't Hooft had called for a closer link between the UBS and the WCC and outlined the need for a joint study. His proposal generated strong support, and Eric North, who had succeeded Berggrav as chairman in 1951, suggested a study on how people used the Bible. Berggrav maintained that while preaching and teaching for people to read the Bible is a concern of the churches, the Bible Societies were also called upon to help people find their way through the Bible. The UBS Study Secretary, Dr. A. M. Chirgwin, had reported wonderful stories about the use of the Bible in evangelism. Berggrav commented, "True it has been proved in some parts of the world that the Bible may be its own best witness. But the European experience points the other way, as we were reminded at the conference in Zurich in 1955 in the question of the Ethiopian to Philip: 'How can I understand, except someone should guide me?' " (Acts 8:31).

From this point on, Berggrav articulated the need for helps in addition to the Bible text "without note or comment." He asked the BFBS to change its constitution, as he had asked the Norwegian Bible Society to change its constitution. "The

Bible Societies," he insisted, "cannot be disinterested in what people do with their Bibles."

He outlined the reason why a second Study Secretary had been appointed.

> Experiments are being made in various countries—Bible Weeks, Bible Campaigns—in which churches and Bible Societies cooperate. But further experiments, further study are needed in which Bible Societies and Churches must cooperate, particularly in some areas where there is a tendency for the activity of the Bible Society to be taken too much for granted (by the churches) as something which *runs of its own accord* as it was expressed in 1949. It is not a question of Bible Societies becoming something like churches or Home Missions, but that from the Bible Society side we should begin helping and perhaps enthusing the local churches, cooperating with them also in producing helpful literature and in colportage, which in many places has been proved to be excellent if well guided. This was our aim in appointing the second Study Secretary as a link between the World Council of Churches, the International Missionary Society and the Bible Societies.

Edwin Robertson was appointed to this office as the second UBS Study Secretary and was given the task of conducting a world study called "The Use of the Bible in the Living Situation of the Churches." Berggrav had insisted that it be based in Geneva and guided by a committee composed of representatives of the United Bible Societies, the International Missionary Council, and the World Council of Churches. He followed it closely and gave enormous support to Robertson's studies, particularly in his own country. When, after his careful guidance, Robertson completed the study of the Use of the Bible of Norway, he read it carefully and commented in typical fashion, "You are right, but you shouldn't publish it, because there are too many Norwegian clergy who read English!"

Berggrav was not able to hear the report of the study to the Third Assembly of the WCC in New Delhi in 1961, yet he followed it as long as he lived, meeting with Robertson often until the last meeting in his cabin at the end of 1958, a month or two before he died. Neither did he live to see the fulfillment of his vision when Bible Societies and Churches met together in Driebergen in 1964. His successor as President, Archbishop Donald Coggan, invited church leaders and Bible Societies to consider their common task, drawing on Berggrav's vision from previous years. But in 1956–57, Berggrav helped the UBS to keep the vision bright. It was not only in the global sphere that he operated, but also in his own Norwegian Bible Society, taking an active part in translation and writing an influential *Letter to Bible Readers*, for new readers, a copy of which was inserted in every Bible distributed by the Norwegian Bible Society.

Last Meeting

In the early days of the UBS, it was obvious that Europe had to be the main area of operation while the larger Bible Societies learned to cooperate through joint agencies. Berggrav had played his part in the changes required in the smaller European societies. But when Béguin looked back at the work of the pioneers, he singled out one aspect of Berggrav's contribution, "Remember Bishop Berggrav's plea, year after year, in the early years of the UBS, that our very name should embody that vision of the worldwide nature of our task."

The first meeting of the UBS Council outside Europe and the United States was in Rio de Janeiro and Sao Paulo, Brazil, during June and July of 1957. Berggrav was in poor physical health, but as Bishop Donald Coggan said, "the inner fires were still burning," adding that they were "the fires of love for his Lord, and of keen interest in the spread of the written word."

The exhilaration of the new country and the widening work of the UBS seemed to restore him at first. His sense of humor was fresh at this meeting at the Colegio Bennett, a girls' school. The participants were cared for enthusiastically, but the accommodations were not always adequate. Berggrav opened the wardrobe in his room and was set upon by a swarm of mosquitoes. This later affected him and he was unable to keep some of his appointments in Sao Paulo.

Berggrav was, however, glad to be there and played his part in the meetings, but he was very weak and ill. Eventually it was decided that Margaret Sullivan, Béguin's secretary, should accompany him home. She reported how ill he had been on the journey back. He died eighteen months later.

MAN OF THE BOOK

Eivind Berggrav died on January 14, 1959, at the age of 74, while drafting a letter to all preachers of the Norwegian Church about a national Bible Sunday in May. The letter was unfinished; among his last written words were:

> Bible Sunday? I have the impression that many of you stop at one problem: it is so difficult for people to get anything out of Bible reading. I myself was hindered by this for a long time, in some way shy when confronted with the Bible. Then I became honest enough to neglect it for a time. People *do* get something out of reading the "difficult book," as was excellently expressed by the African woman who said, "This book *reads me.*"

> Next: there are so many great and good causes in which we ask the congregation to take interest. Offerings are not popular. But *this* cause, the Bible mission, sending the Bible out to all people and tribes, has priority, because it concerns the basis of all Christianity, and because it is urgent just now... .

There his strength failed and he wrote no more.

The *UBS Bulletin* for the second half of 1984 was headed, *Bishop Eivind Berggrav—A Centenary.* It contained an account of Berggrav's life, his speeches and sermons, and at the end, a series of personal tributes. One is by Bill Platt, General Secretary of the British and Foreign Bible Society, 1947–61, who had previously written a tribute to Berggrav on his death in 1959. Platt's words were—and remain today—a suitable summary of the relationship between Berggrav and the United Bible Societies.

> Bishop Berggrav was the first president of the UBS and I well remember the light in the eyes of my predecessor at the London Bible House, John Temple, when in 1946 he returned from a visit to Oslo. He had gone there to seek the Bishop's interest in the work of drawing the Bible Societies closer together into one fellowship and to recruit Dr. Berggrav's help in rousing some of the older Societies on the Continent into real missionary Bible Society work. Temple returned to London quite triumphant, sure that the Bishop was prepared to lead. He was not mistaken, for from the very first the Bishop's ecumenical contacts, spiritual insight, forthrightness, dedication and keen sense of humour were ours, and they remained so to the very day of his death.

Berggrav's ecumenical stature, his scholarship, and his battles for realism in life and religion were widely acknowledged after his death. Here is a final testimony:

> We, in the London Bible House, remember him as a lover of the BFBS and as a father in God. When a place for the Headquarters of the UBS was under discussion, it was Berggrav's voice, which finally decided the question: should it be Geneva, New York or London? "For us in Scandinavia" he said, quite briefly, "London has always been the center of Bible work and if you would carry us with you, London it must be." And London it was! To Scotland, Germany, Switzerland, France, the United States, and even Rio de Janeiro, Bishop Berggrav came with us, ever lending his international prestige to this work, ever spicing our solemn sessions with his sly humor, the penetrating vision, the realistic thrust which time and again kept our feet on the ground. Many will remember him best for his searching addresses at the end of our conferences. For others, his outstanding leadership to over a score of Bible

Societies, now joined in close-knit cooperation, will stand out as his greatest gift to us.

CONCLUSION

Eivind Berggrav's courage and ingenuity in resisting the Quisling regime during the Nazi occupation of Norway will long be remembered in his native land. Yet his life and ministry extended both before and after those tumultuous years of World War II. All his experiences prior to the outbreak of war prepared him in character and faith for that crucial time. His faith was forged in the midst of honest doubt. His character developed as he grasped a faith that was his own—not inherited, but shaped and strengthened by God in the middle of strife. His ruthless analysis of himself, his acceptance of personal weaknesses and mistakes, his readiness to understand those with whom he disagreed, and his growing skills at reconciling those who differed on various issues combined to make a man devoted to God's truth and the dignity of human beings.

Although he often sat alone while under house arrest in his cabin at Asker, Berggrav had remarkably rich resources for his faith: God's Word, the Holy Scriptures which he read and meditated on daily, and the writings of Martin Luther and the Confessions of the Lutheran Church. These two treasures provided the strength he needed to resist. The Gospel, the heart of Scripture and the Lutheran Confessions, moved him to care for the church in Norway and around the world. God's mercy also motivated him to be in mission to *all* people. Equipped by divine grace, he sought to listen more carefully and to understand more fully those utterly opposed to him.

No better example of this trait can be found than his final visit to Vidkun Quisling. Condemned to death as a traitor, Quisling protested that he was not a traitor, but had always acted out of love for his country. Berggrav believed him, yet he was also vocal in criticizing Quisling's misuse of power and the atrocities he had allowed during his regime. In this prison cell on October 16, 1945, Berggrav and Quisling did not discuss the war, national policies, or their past conflicts; the conversation revolved around *eternal* matters. Berggrav the pastor was counseling a man about to meet his Maker. The Bishop reminded Quisling that no one knows the moment when they will be stand before God for judgment, but in the face of death, we have opportunity to prepare ourselves. "Let us pray the Lord's Prayer," he advised, focusing especially on the words, "Forgive us our trespasses, as we forgive those who trespass against us." In those moments together, Berggrav and Quisling spoke of reconciliation and forgiveness, made possible by the death of God's Son for the sins of the world. The Bishop and pastor shared with the prisoner that in life's darkest moments the love of God in Christ shines with hope and life.

After his visit, Berggrav wrote the Prime Minister to ask for clemency to Quisling. The appeal was without effect. The people of Norway demanded the death penalty. Quisling was executed by firing squad.

Years later as his own death drew near, Eivind Berggrav found comfort in the light of the Gospel and the ministry of the church. He had devoted his life to the task of reconciling churches and nations and to the work of bringing the Scriptures to peoples around the world. He served as shepherd and prophet to his country and Europe. He was a builder of bridges among divided populations and continents. He was Bishop of Norway, but beyond his particular calling Berggrav was a witness for Christ to the whole church. To the end he remained a servant of the Lord, standing firm against spiritual foes on God's eternal promises.